D0432360

FOR THE LOVE OF

FOOTBALL

HERTFORDSHIRE LIBRARY SERVICE

WITHDRAWN FOR SALE

FOR THE LOVE OF FOOTBALL

First published as The Joy of Football in 2014

This revised and expanded edition copyright © Summersdale Publishers Ltd, 2017

All rights reserved.

No part of this book may be reproduced by any means, nor transmitted, nor translated into a machine language, without the written permission of the publishers.

Johnny Morgan has asserted his right to be identified as the author of this work in accordance with sections 77 and 78 of the Copyright, Designs and Patents Act 1988.

Condition of Sale
This book is sold subject to the condition that it shall not, by way of trade or otherwise, be lent, resold, hired out or otherwise circulated in any form of binding or cover other than that in which it is published and without a similar condition including this condition being imposed on the subsequent purchaser.

Summersdale Publishers Ltd
46 West Street
Chichester
West Sussex
PO19 1RP
UK

www.summersdale.com

Printed and bound in the Czech Republic

ISBN: 978-1-78685-009-6

Substantial discounts on bulk quantities of Summersdale books are available to corporations, professional associations and other organisations. For details contact general enquiries: telephone: +44 (0) 1243 771107, fax: +44 (0) 1243 786300 or email: enquiries@summersdale.com.

FOR THE LOVE OF
FOOTBALL

A COMPANION

JOHNNY MORGAN

summersdale

For Tom. And for Dad.

CONTENTS

....

INTRODUCTION

· ·

Football makes people do strange things. It makes me do strange things. Things that non-addicted souls would look at and ask 'but why?' And, like true addicts, we do these things over and over again, always chasing the next hit. We do them for the love of football.

Still now, I turn up for games of football in the depths of winter, when anyone with a firmer grip on their sanity would stay inside. The thermometer might well be below zero and the snow might be piled up around the pitch but, if the pitch is playable and everyone is ready to go, then so am I.

I once dragged myself up before dawn, jumped on flights across Europe and stayed in a stranger's spare room to see a European Cup final contested by two teams, neither of which I supported. The atmosphere was electric but the game was dreadful.

As a child, I insisted to my parents that wearing a full football kit and drawing on a moustache was a suitable costume for fancy dress parties. I spent my last pennies on football stickers, forgoing chocolate and sweets. Week after week, in the pursuit of completed sticker books. I've repeated this behaviour as an adult, pretending when someone asks that the stickers are for my not-yet-old-enough son.

There are plenty of other stories. The point is that football has ended up mapping out my life. For example, I can remember as a nine-year-old the excitement of staying up late with my dad to watch Liverpool v Roma in the European Cup final, hooked on every second and mesmerised by Grobbelaar's wobbly legs. Fast forward a couple of years and just back from an eye-opening school trip to France, a new feeling of utter despair was gripping me as I watched Maradona's hand and feet knock England out of the World Cup.

Then there was sneaking off to see AFC Bournemouth play Manchester United in the fifth round of the FA Cup in 1989. We had to be secretive on that February day because dad had only two tickets, so we couldn't let my brother know what we were doing. A little over 11 years later, I was playing football on a Brazilian beach. A side of 20-something Brits overcame a bunch of younger locals thanks to the triumph of organisation and passing over flair and determined yet doomed dribbling. Jump to 2015 and, with my fifth decade approaching, I was on another beach, with my brother, witnessing my local club's greatest ever moment. After an entire history spent in the lower leagues, the Cherries had won promotion to the promised land of the Premier League and were celebrating on Bournemouth sands. A historic day that was one of my dad's very last.

I'm pretty certain this happens the world over: lives wrapped in football. I have the good fortune to play football every week with guys from every corner of the earth. They all have football moments that they will never forget. You'll find their stories scattered throughout the book. This is mine:

FOOTBALL MOMENT

I don't remember much about the first 112 minutes of England's game against Belgium at the 1990 World Cup. And watching the game back, I'm not surprised. It was a turgid match with Belgium providing most of the barely memorable moments. They should have won. But with the game heading to penalties, in the 113th minute, substitute David Platt, a relative unknown to this viewer, scored a sensational volley to win it. England fans went mad, including a bunch of football-mad 15-year-olds crowded round a small television in a friend's bedroom. It was a moment of uncontrolled joy, which looking back was so joyful because it was laced with an enormous dose of disbelief. I didn't realise it at the time, but you don't get many of these.

Johnny, England

A BRIEF HISTORY
OF FOOTBALL

· ·

Playing football is very simple, but playing simple football is the hardest thing there is.

DUTCH FOOTBALL LEGEND JOHAN CRUYFF

When did it all begin? Who gets credit for inventing the beautiful game? Well, that isn't entirely clear. There's mention of *tsu chu*, involving a leather ball filled with feathers and hair, in China around 200 BC; *kemari*, which featured players standing in a small circle trying to keep the ball off the ground, in Japan in AD 600; *episkyros*, a much more physical pursuit than its Far Eastern equivalent, at roughly the same time in Greece; something called Shrovetide football, akin to mob football where hands were used as much as feet, in the Middle Ages in England; and *calcio*, comprising 27 players whose focus was fighting as much as football, in Italy in the 1500s. Let's just say it's a global game. But one thing is certain: the modern game, as we know it, was born in 1863 and the fun hasn't stopped since.

A TIMELINE OF MODERN FOOTBALL

1862   Notts County, the oldest professional football club, is formed

1863   The rules of Association Football are drawn up in England

1869   Goal kicks are introduced to the game

1870   The position of goalkeeper is officially recognised

1872   Corner kicks are introduced to the game

1872   The first international takes place: Scotland plays England

1874   Shin pads are introduced and teams change ends at half-time

1877   The duration of a match is set at 90 minutes

1890   Goal nets are used for the first time

1891   Penalty kicks are introduced

1893   The first three-figure transfer: Willie Groves to Aston Villa for £100

1904   Fédération Internationale de Football Association (FIFA) is founded in Paris

1923   The first Football Association (FA) Cup final at Wembley: Bolton v West Ham

1930   The first World Cup takes place in Uruguay

1937   Football is televised for the first time: highlights of Arsenal v Arsenal Reserves

1939   Shirt numbering becomes compulsory

1951   The use of a white ball is permitted for the first time

1960   The European Championship is founded

1960   The first live English Football League game is broadcast on TV

1965   Substitutions are permitted in the English Football League

1970   The game sees its first red and yellow cards

1979   Trevor Francis becomes the first British £1-million footballer

1991   The first women's football World Cup takes place in China

1992   The English Premier League is born

1992   The Champions League replaces the European Cup

2002   The World Cup takes place in Asia for the first time

2010   The World Cup is held in Africa for the first time

2012   Goal-line technology is first used

2014   Vanishing spray and goal-line technology make their debut at the World Cup

2016   A fourth substitute in extra time is trialled in the Copa América final and at the 2016 Olympic Games

2016   Goal-line technology is introduced for all European Champions League games

2016   Video refereeing is trialled in an international friendly between France and Italy

2017   An additional substitute is allowed in extra time in the quarter-finals, semi-finals and final of the FA Cup in England

2018   FIFA hopes that the World Cup in Russia will be the first tournament to see video referees help on-pitch officials with 'game-changing' decisions

A LEVEL PLAYING FIELD

While football had existed in various forms for centuries, it wasn't very organised. Steps had to be taken to turn the chaos into something more cultured, into a spectacle that was fairer, and whose joy could be shared far and wide. Association Football was the result, with the first laws drawn up in 1863 with the purpose of 'embracing the true principles of the game, with the greatest simplicity'.

WHEN PRESTON RULED THE WORLD

The first football league competition was held in England between the autumn of 1888 and the spring of 1889, and Preston North End dominated it completely. The Lilywhites, as their fans call them, were on top of the world – they were invincible, unbeaten over the entire 22-game season. They won the year after, too. Since then, things haven't been quite so good, but they'll always have that season in the sun.

And what a season it was. It took until 2003–2004 for another team, Arsenal, to emulate Preston and go a whole

English Football League season without loss. The Gunners had to play nearly twice as many games, but let's not get bogged down in detail. The Lilywhites were one of the 12 founding fathers of the league and you can only beat what's put in front of you, and that they did. They put seven past Stoke City and five past Burnley, Derby County, and Wolverhampton Wanderers at home, and seven past Brighton & Hove Albion on the road. Two Preston players led the top scorers' table, with John Goodall just pipping teammate James Ross thanks to a goal-a-game record.

Incredibly, Preston won the FA Cup in the same season, becoming the first English team to claim the coveted Double. They did it without conceding a goal, too: they rattled three past Bootle, two past Grimsby Town, two more past Birmingham City and one past West Bromwich Albion, before beating Wolves 3–0 in the final at the Kennington Oval in London in front of over 27,000 fans. How do the Arsenal Invincibles compare? They lost in the semi-finals. Close, but no cigar.

England manager Alf Ramsey to striker Rodney Marsh:
If you don't work harder I'll pull you off at half-time.

Soon to be ex-England striker to manager Alf Ramsey:
Crikey, Alf, at Manchester City all we get is an orange and a cup of tea.

THE SECOND COMING

Talk to fans of a certain age group and you'd think that football didn't exist before the advent of the Premier League. Before this juggernaut came rumbling into view, there was just darkness, lurking in which were horrors such as really short shorts, mullets and limited media coverage.

It's not true, obviously, but the Premier League did usher in a new era of football and, with the help of a sports channel belonging to a certain Australian media tycoon, turned it into the behemoth we look upon today. And it's not just a British we: visit virtually any city in the world and you'll spot the shirts of Manchester United, Liverpool, Arsenal, Chelsea and others. There's a reason for that: the rise and rise of the Premier League.

Before 1992, watching football on television wasn't always so easy. The number of televised games was limited to one or two a week, if you were lucky, and as far as highlights went, you had to pay attention to the listings and hunt down specific programmes at certain times to get a glimpse of the action. And if your team was playing in the week, watching the match took some serious dedication and the ability to stay up late (past the greyhound racing and showjumping). You couldn't just turn on the box and breezily flick around until you found something you wanted to watch. Four or five top-flight games over a weekend? *Soccer Saturday*? *Super Sunday*? *Monday Night Football*? For that kind of joy you had to wait for the World Cup.

The make-up of English football has changed in other ways since the arrival of the Premier League. The extra money has enabled more and more domestic clubs to look further afield for talent and they have grabbed this opportunity with both hands: the league now has the second-largest proportion of overseas players in Europe (Cyprus is first). The merits of this evolution are much debated: for all the Cantonas, Zolas, Henrys and Bergkamps, there are the Boogerses, Bogardes, Bebés and Brolins. Furthermore, the England team hasn't been much cop of late, a decline which some argue is a result of the lack of opportunity for young home-grown players. Nevertheless, it has created an insatiable appetite around the world for the league.

Talking of hunger, the influx of Premier League riches means that today top footballers become millionaires almost overnight. Not too long ago, the footballing wage was largely a modest one: in 1958, the maximum a footballer could earn was £20 a week; now Wayne Rooney gets paid £300,000 a week. Transfer fees have also gone through the ceiling: from £1 million for Trevor Francis in 1979 to £93.2 million for Paul Pogba in 2016. And let's not forget other Premier League moves such as £59.7 million for Ángel Di María, £51 million for Kevin De Bruyne, £50 million for Fernando Torres, £49 million for Raheem Sterling, £47 million for John Stones, £44 million for Mesut Özil and £39.5 million for Sergio Agüero.

So, in a way, 1992 was year zero: before that it was a game that a lot of fans would no longer recognise.

WHAT A GOAL!

- The first Premier League goal was scored by Brian Deane for Sheffield United against Manchester United in 1992. The Blades beat the Red Devils 2–1.

- The 10,000th Premier League goal was scored by Les Ferdinand for Tottenham Hotspur against Fulham in 2001.

- The 20,000th Premier League goal was scored by Marc Albrighton for Aston Villa against Arsenal in 2011.

- The 24,000th Premier League goal was scored by Kieran Gibbs for Arsenal against Tottenham in 2015.

93.2

The most expensive player in the world is Paul Pogba. Manchester United signed the French international from Juventus in August 2016 for £93.2 million, topping the £86 million Real Madrid paid Tottenham for Gareth Bale in 2013. The Italian side made a very healthy profit on the midfielder: he cost them just £800,000 in 2012. Where did he come from? Manchester United.

THE LANGUAGE OF FOOTBALL

··

> **❝** *If that had gone in, it would have been a goal.* **❞**
> LEGENDARY FOOTBALL COMMENTATOR DAVID COLEMAN

Watch a few games, or spend some time contemplating the post-match analysis of ex-pro pundits, and it quickly becomes clear that football has its own language. There may be a trend towards more intelligible commentary – stand up Gary Neville and Danny Murphy, among others – but there's still no escaping the unique, often illogical vernacular. For newcomers, there's a lot to translate. Here's a start.

A BACK FOUR

This is a reference to a team's defensive players when it is playing four of them. Normally a back four comprises a right back, two centre backs and a left back. However, sides can also play with three or five defenders (a back three or a back five).

A SWEET LEFT FOOT

This isn't a reference to a foot that generally conducts its affair in a good-hearted way. Or one that tastes sugary. It means that the owner is capable of displaying an above-average level of skill with said foot.

A SITTER

A sitter is a really easy opportunity to score a goal and is normally preceded by the words 'missed a' in reference to a player's failure to take this simplest of chances. Is there any sitting down involved? Well, the fans may feel that the player might serve their team best if they take a seat on the bench.

BACKS AGAINST THE WALL

Teams are often said to have their backs against the wall. There are no physical walls to speak of. The term refers to a side that is being put under a lot of pressure by their opponents and having to defend desperately.

BOOK HIM!

Not for a shampoo advert, a reality TV programme or an after-dinner speaking gig. When someone shouts (and it is usually shouted) 'book him!' they want the referee to give the player in question a yellow card. To do so involves the referee writing the player's name in their book.

BURY IT!

If you hear this at a game, it isn't an instruction to dig a hole and put the ball in it. If a fan is shouting this, they are imploring a player to score a goal. Commentators are often heard to say, 'He should have buried it,' when referring to a missed chance.

BUSINESS END OF THE SEASON

This term refers to the last month or so of a domestic football season. This is the time when teams win trophies, achieve promotion, qualify for European competitions and suffer relegation. This is the business that's happening.

DEAD BALL SPECIALIST

Not an expert in rendering balls lifeless or any kind of footballing sadist, but a player who excels at taking and scoring penalties and free kicks or can deliver a corner kick with pinpoint accuracy. A dead ball is one that isn't moving.

FALSE NINE

A false nine is a football player: a real one rather than an opportunistic fan that has somehow got themselves in a team line-up. The term refers to a striker who drops deep into midfield rather than playing in the traditional centre-forward position further up the pitch.

FERGIE TIME

Sir Alex Ferguson may have retired but Fergie time lives on. When a generous or excessive amount of time has been added to injury time at the end of a game and a team scores in this period, they are often said to have scored in Fergie time.

HAT-TRICK

There's no one pulling a rabbit out of a hat here. In fact, there are no hats or tricks at all. This term is used when a player scores three goals in the same match. After scoring a hat-trick, the player usually gets to take the ball home.

3

For a defender to score a hat-trick is eye-catching in itself, yet when West Ham United centre back Alvin Martin bagged a trio of goals in a league game against Newcastle in 1986 he did something even more incredible: he scored past three different goalkeepers. The No. 1s (official and emergency) were Martin Thomas, Chris Hedworth and Peter Beardsley.

HANDBAGS

If you hear mention of 'handbags' in relation to a football game, it doesn't mean anyone is sporting the latest designs from Lulu Guinness, Gucci, etc. It means two players are involved in a fight that isn't really a fight – shouting and pointing rather than punching.

HIT THE WOODWORK

There's no violence towards misshapen pencil cases of our school days here, although something does normally get a good whack. When you hear this it means a player has struck the post or crossbar with the ball. The frame of the goal used to be made of wood – hence, woodwork.

HOSPITAL PASS

This is a pass no player wants. It is an under-hit pass that subjects the recipient to a potentially bone-crunching tackle, usually unavoidable, from an opponent that could send either player to A & E.

HUGGING THE LINE

When wingers stay close to the edge of the pitch, or the touchline, when playing, they are said to be hugging the line. Players are often encouraged to do so in an attempt to stretch the game and gain an advantage over opponents. Any bromance is incidental.

MAN ON!

Not a reference to the famous ballet or an instruction to lift someone rugby-style high into the air, but a warning, normally delivered at a high volume by either a teammate or the crowd, to a player in possession of the ball that an opponent is fast approaching and a tackle is imminent.

NUTMEG

If you hear the shout 'megs!' during a football game, this is no culinary reference. The nutmeg – rolling the ball between an opponent's legs and collecting it the other side – is one of the most humiliating tricks someone can pull on a football field. It is also one of the most enjoyable.

PARK THE BUS

There are no actual buses or parking involved here. When a team is said to have parked the bus it means that they have adopted an ultra-defensive strategy that involves doing anything to stop the opposition scoring a goal.

PRAWN SANDWICH BRIGADE

This is a slur coined by the famously combustible Roy Keane. The prawn sandwich brigade is a group of fans that attend games essentially to enjoy corporate hospitality (including said snacks) rather than to support a team. They lack passion and commitment.

PUT IT IN THE MIXER

Nothing to do with cement or food, though it's all about an end product. The mixer on this occasion is the penalty area and the instruction here is to play a long ball into it in the hope a striker might score.

ROUTE ONE

When a team plays route one football it means they are trying to score goals by kicking long, high balls towards their opponent's goal. This unsophisticated strategy is not held in very high regard but is often used to good effect.

ROW Z

A player can always find Row Z even if a ground isn't big enough to have such a tier. If a striker hits Row Z with a shot it means that their attempt has sailed so far over the top of the goal that it will reach the furthermost row of seating.

SHANK

There's no lamb involved here, but maybe a dog. A dog's dinner to be precise. When you hear the term in football it means a player has woefully miskicked the ball, sending it in completely the wrong direction.

FOOTIE FACT

The longest team name in football belongs to Dutch side Nooit Opgeven Altijd Doorzetten Aangenaam Door Vermaak En Nuttig Door Ontspanning Combinatie Breda, whose title comprises 86 letters. They are more commonly known as NAC Breda. Also worth a mention are Welsh side Clwb Pêl-droed Llanfairpwllgwyngyllgogerychwyrndrobwllllantysiliogogogoch (70 letters) and German club Verein für Leibesübungen Borussia Mönchengladbach (45 letters).

SQUARE IT!

There's no square to talk of here, just a straight-ish line. This is an instruction to pass the ball sideways across the pitch to a player in a more advantageous position. Sometimes it is heeded, sometimes it is not.

SQUEAKY BUM TIME

This is the time at the end of a game when one team is hanging on, often desperately, for the final whistle and the result they need. Usually a matter of minutes, this period is normally extremely tense and hugely exciting.

TIKI-TAKA

Not a colourful child's game or tapas dish, but a style of playing football based on keeping possession by means of highly accurate short passing and movement. Not a new phenomenon but has been big recently in Spain. Now suffering something of a backlash.

TOE PUNT

When a footballer uses the end of his or her boot, rather than the laces or instep, to take a shot at goal, it's called a toe punt, or toe poke. This method of striking a ball is often maligned as rudimentary and unsophisticated, yet it can be highly effective.

TOTAL FOOTBALL

This is football at its most fluid: an attack-orientated style of playing in which players can swap positions at will. Defenders can play as forwards and vice-a-versa. The most famous proponent of this sublime strategy was Dutch footballing master Johan Cruyff.

UNDER THE COSH

When a football team is said to be under the cosh, the players aren't being beaten viciously by an opposing side or fans. Instead, the team is being put under severe pressure by their opponents and having to defend almost without pause.

VOTE OF CONFIDENCE

There's not always a vote involved and often there's little confidence to be clung to. If a manager on a bad losing streak is given one of these by their chairman, it usually means that he'll be sacked shortly. Hence, this phrase is often preceded by the words 'the dreaded'.

WET WEDNESDAY NIGHT IN STOKE

This phrase is often heard in following context: 'But can they do it on a cold wet Wednesday night in Stoke?' This is a question often asked of foreign players, usually those from warmer climes. It doesn't have to be a Wednesday or Stoke; the implied criticism is that the player will struggle against a physical side away from home in difficult conditions.

29

Scottish football fans are used to games being postponed because of bad weather, but in 1979 supporters of Falkirk and Inverness Thistle had to wait a very long time to see their teams play a Scottish Cup tie. Originally scheduled for 6 January, the match wasn't decided until 22 February, some 47 days later. It was cancelled a record-breaking 29 times. Falkirk eventually won 4–0.

They're the second best team in the world, and there's no higher praise than that.

KEVIN KEEGAN

THE WORLD CUP

> *Good afternoon. Shouldn't you be at work?*
>
> BBC PRESENTER DES LYNAM'S FIRST WORDS TO THE CAMERA WHEN INTRODUCING ENGLAND'S GAME AGAINST TUNISIA AT THE 1998 WORLD CUP. KICK-OFF TIME? 2 P.M.

The English Premier League, La Liga in Spain, the Bundesliga in Germany, the UEFA Champions League: they have the football, the stars, the glamour and the money, but the World Cup still trumps them all. For one month every four years, the world eats, sleeps and breathes football.

THE WORLD CUP BEGINS

Unsurprisingly the World Cup has changed a lot since its grand launch in 1930. The inaugural tournament in Uruguay bears little resemblance to the meticulously organised, super-sponsored competitions we consume today. For a start, teams were hardly falling over themselves to play. For all the success of the Olympic football tournaments in the 1920s and the efforts of FIFA President Jules Rimet, who threw all his energy behind creating a global competition for his organisation, no one wanted to take part. It's fair to say that the World Cup got off to a slow start.

Everyone at FIFA got excited when the competition was announced, two years before when invitations were sent out. So far so good. Except FIFA hadn't counted on a somewhat sniffy reaction from Europe's football associations. Initially, everyone said thanks, but no thanks. The cost of travel was the widely cited excuse, but the reason for the lacklustre response wasn't entirely financial: the Home Nations were mired in a period of arch snobbery and felt the competition was beneath them.

Eventually some arm-twisting from Rimet resulted in four teams making the trip: Belgium, France, Romania and Yugoslavia. They joined Argentina, Bolivia, Brazil, Chile, Mexico, Paraguay, Peru and the USA, as well as the host, Uruguay, who were all, unsurprisingly, keener to make the much shorter journey. The tournament was played by 13 teams across three venues, all in the capital Montevideo, and comprised 18 games, with Uruguay defeating Argentina 2–1 in the final, 17 days after the first ball had been kicked. Compare this with the 2018 World Cup in Russia: 32 teams, 12 venues across a very large country, 65 games and 31 days.

It would take a while before the English FA got over themselves, the South Americans got over being snubbed by the Europeans (there were retaliatory boycotts in 1934 and 1938) and teams stopped pulling out for sometimes spurious reasons ('Olympic football is more important', 'We don't want to wear football boots', etc.). But by 1982 the World Cup had been expanded to 24 teams and in 1998 to 32, by which time the tournament was truly a global affair that everyone took seriously.

Will the World Cup get any bigger? Arguably it doesn't need to, but common sense has long been out of fashion when considering such things. A 48-team tournament has been approved by FIFA and there's talk of making it even larger.

FOOTIE FACT

Brazil became the fifth country to host the World Cup for a second time in 2014, following Italy (1934 and 1990), France (1938 and 1998), Mexico (1970 and 1986) and Germany (1974 as West Germany and 2006).

36.8

The FIFA World Cup Trophy is 36.8 centimetres high and weighs 6.1 kilograms. It replaced the Abel Lafleur-designed Jules Rimet Trophy, which was given to Brazil in 1970 when they completed a hat-trick of tournaments. The old trophy was slightly smaller (35 centimetres) and significantly lighter (3.8 kilograms).

THE WINNERS TAKE IT ALL

Winning and losing. The joy of victory and the fear of defeat. What else is the World Cup, or indeed any football tournament about? That's why we watch, even if it means getting up in the middle of the night or pleading with the boss to get out of work early.

When it comes to being joyful, it's the Brazilian fans who have the most reasons to be happy, not just because of the way their team play the game (or used to at least), but because they've walked off with football's ultimate crown a record five times. Plus they're the only side to win it on four different continents.

Of course Brazil isn't the only team to have multiple World Cup notches on its bedpost. Argentina and Uruguay have both won it twice, while Germany and Italy can boast four victories each. And it shouldn't be forgotten that England, France and Spain have all brought the big one home once. Notably, England and France were both victorious as hosts and history has shown that putting on the party does improve your chances. Apart from the home victories in 1966 and 1998, the hosts have won it on four other occasions. That's not a bad ratio; still, Qatari fans shouldn't get too excited about 2022.

FOOTIE FACT

The heaviest defeat suffered at a World Cup? Hungary beat El Salvador 10–1 in Spain in 1982. South Korea (who lost 9–0 to Hungary in 1954) and Zaire (who lost 9–0 to Yugoslavia in 1974) probably felt just as bad.

FOOTBALL MOMENT

It was the 1994 World Cup. In a post-communist regime Romania, people were gathering in front of the buildings where they were living and where the owner of the nearest convenience store or bar was making special arrangements for this occasion by setting up plenty of seats and a TV where everybody was gathering each night for the football games. The moment when Romania scored the golden goal against Argentina in the Round of 16 was one of great joy. Qualifying for a historical quarter-final crystallized all of Romania's strengths in that tournament. I will never forget that tournament and the matches. It was a place full of emotion, hope, strengthening communities and joy.

Bogdan, Romania

FOOTIE FACT

The 22-man Republic of Ireland squad for the 1990 World Cup included just six players actually born in the country. Striker Niall Quinn, one of those born in Ireland, was also registered as the team's third goalkeeper.

STAR LIGHT, STAR BRIGHT

Who are the stars of the World Cup? OK, we might remember how the likes of Franz Beckenbauer (he of God-like status, if you're German, and maybe even if you're not), Roger Milla (him of Cameroon and the fancy dance) and Gazza (oh the skill, oh the tears) lit up tournaments in their time, but when it comes down to it, it's the goals that count, and in particular the players who scored the most.

Beckenbauer and Milla may have notched up a fair few goals between them (both with a very respectable five), but the daddy of hitting the back of net at the World Cup is Miroslav Klose.

He banged in 16 goals for Germany, which is one more than Ronaldo (not the new, slick version, but the older, cuddlier one). Behind these guys are Just Fontaine of France, with 13, and Pelé, with 12.

So, does being a top World Cup goalscorer make you one of the best of all time? Quite possibly, but such a judgement is perhaps an impossible one to make. To score a goal in a World Cup you have to actually be there: there are plenty of players whose skills are lauded as some of the best the sport has seen, but who have never graced the game's ultimate tournament.

Take George Best for instance. For all his proclivities off the field, on it he was near peerless. But, as a Northern Irishman, his opportunities to prove himself on the biggest stage were next to none. Ryan Giggs is another player whose mercurial skills were never given the World Cup showcase they deserved. His Wales teams toiled away at qualification but could never drag themselves over the finishing line, even with the help of their Welsh Wizard.

Of course, such fate is not solely a British phenomenon. European football has its own stories of this type of poor fortune, and none perhaps as unfortunate as that of Alfredo Di Stéfano. Di Stéfano is a footballing god, grouped by many among the game's very best (we're talking Pelé, Maradona and Messi territory here). The reason, perhaps, why he isn't automatically included at this top table is because he never played in a World Cup. It wasn't for lack of trying, although it was arguably the trying that did for him. Before he even arrived at Real Madrid in 1953, where he went on to win five European Cups, the Argentinian striker had already turned out for his native country and Colombia. A mixture of non-qualification, withdraws and bans kept him from World Cups. So, he switched his allegiance to Spain (who knows what was going on at FIFA), but Scotland (yes, Scotland) blocked his path in 1958 and he was injured in 1962. And that was it: three countries and no World Cup.

The book on such players can't be closed without mention of George Weah. He was another sublimely gifted player – the 1995 FIFA World Player of the Year – from Liberia. As far as World Cups go that's a major problem right there. Can you name another Liberian player? Exactly. Liberia has never come close to qualification and neither did poor old George.

FOOTIE FACT

Robert Prosinečki is the only player to have scored World Cup goals for two different countries: for Yugoslavia in 1990 and Croatia in 1998.

FOOTIE FACT

Every World Cup final starting line-up since 1982 has included at least one player from German club Bayern Munich:

1982 Breitner, Dremmler and Rummenigge (West Germany)

1986 Matthäus and Eder (West Germany)

1990 Augenthaler and Kohler (West Germany)

1994 Jorginho (Brazil)

1998 Lizarazu (France)

2002 Kahn, Linke and Jeremies (Germany)

2006 Sagnol (France)

2010 Robben and van Bommel (Netherlands)

2014 Neuer, Boateng, Lahm, Schweinsteiger, Kroos and Müller (Germany)

You know, Jack, life for us will never be the same again.

SIR BOBBY CHARLTON, TO HIS BROTHER AND FELLOW WORLD CUP WINNER, JACK, AFTER THE FINAL WHISTLE OF THE 1966 FINAL BETWEEN ENGLAND AND WEST GERMANY

WE AREN'T
THE CHAMPIONS

· ·

In Spain, all 22 players make the sign of the cross before a game; if it worked, every game would be a tie.
DUTCH TIKI-TAKA PIONEER JOHAN CRUYFF

Football only remembers the winners. But sometimes the gallant losers, the silver medallists, the number twos are worth celebrating too.

THE MIGHTY MAGYARS

To label the Hungarian national team of the 1950s as serial second-placers is unfair and not really true. But this golden team, led by one of the footballing greats Ferenc Puskás, is remembered as the best team never to win the World Cup.

Their chance came at the 1954 tournament in Switzerland and they were widely expected to win the trophy. Having refused to take part in the 1950 competition, Hungary had gone on an extraordinary winning run that would change football forever. They took home Olympic gold in 1952, won the Central European Championship, a precursor to the European Championship, in 1953, and swept away the foundations of English football with a pair of thrashings in 1953 and 1954.

Puskás' men turned up at the World Cup unbeaten and in imperious form, playing a revolutionary style of football. They waltzed through their group games, which included a walloping of West Germany, survived a brutal quarter-final against Brazil and outplayed reigning champions Uruguay in the semi-final. The final was a rematch against an already beaten West German side.

However, physically spent and carrying an injured Puskás, Hungary couldn't repeat their earlier feats and succumbed to their opponents 3–2 in a game that subsequently became known as the Miracle of Berne. It would be this Hungary side's only defeat in six years, before, in 1956 in the wake of the Hungarian Uprising, the team broke up.

CRUYFF'S NEARLY MEN

That the Dutch national team didn't win a major international trophy in the 1970s is frankly astonishing. This was a team that transformed the game with its Total Football, playing with an elegance and fluidity that would turn the sport on its head, and was led by none other than Johan Cruyff, a footballing master who sits alongside Pelé and Maradona in the pantheon of the world's greatest players.

Their first opportunity to claim global glory came at the 1974 World Cup and they came tantalisingly close to winning the country's first piece of proper football silverware. Cruyff dazzled and turned, almost too much in the end. Leading the hosts West Germany in the final, the Dutch put on a dizzying display of football – all that was missing was an end product. The West Germans duly took advantage and won.

Next up was Euro 76, which was Holland's debut at the competition. They were strongly fancied but they lost their semi-final against Czechoslovakia in a crazy game that featured one own goal, two periods of extra time and three red cards, and was played in torrential rain.

The team's last shot at glory in that decade came at the 1978 World Cup. With their talisman Cruyff not travelling with the squad, Holland weren't expected to replicate their performance in West Germany, but once again they found themselves in a final against the hosts, this time Argentina. Once again, they fell at the last hurdle, underdone in front of a hostile Buenos Aires crowd by the brilliance of Mario Kempes.

FOOTIE FACT

English team Plymouth Argyle finished second in Division Three South six years in a row in the 1920s. The Pilgrims were runners-up in 1921–1922, 1922–1923, 1923–1924, 1924–1925, 1925–1926 and 1926–1927. With only the champions stepping up a league, Plymouth missed out on promotion six times.

THE ALBICELESTES AND THE AGONY

Argentina have won a hatful of major trophies but the last time they did so was in 1993. For a footballing superpower that gap is an eternity. Since successfully defending the Copa América in Ecuador, a country that has been able to count on the likes of Diego Maradona, Hernàn Crespo, Gabriel Batistuta and Lionel Messi, has experienced nothing but heartbreak.

Not since Batistuta fired his team to glory in the 1993 Copa América final against Mexico have Argentine hands touched a trophy that matters. The World Cup has been a barren hunting ground for La Albicelestes. Maradona's drug-taking did for them in 1994, while a group stage flop in 2002 split a string of quarter-final defeats in 1998, 2006 and 2010. In 2014, Argentina would return to final for the first time since 1990. The opponents were the same, give or take a reunification, and so was the result, a 1–0 loss.

The Copa América, South America's equivalent of the European Championship, has been the source of no less anguish for Argentina. The victory in 1993 propelled the country to a record 14th title, but they have yet to add to it. Since this date, four finals have been played and lost, including the centennial tournament to Chile in 2016. Agonisingly, three of these showpieces were lost on penalties. To add salt to an already incredibly sore wound, Argentina's profligacy has allowed Uruguay to overtake them as the region's most successful side in the competition. Ouch.

THE CURSE OF BÉLA GUTTMAN

It was late spring 1962 and Hungarian coach Béla Guttmann had just delivered back-to-back European Cup wins for Portuguese side Benfica, the second of which against continental superpower Real Madrid. Not a bad time to go to the board of directors and ask for a raise. Somewhat surprisingly they said no. Somewhat unsurprisingly Guttman told them where to stick their job. Among the choice words he had for his now former bosses was a scathing prediction that 'not in a hundred years from now will Benfica ever be European champion'.

At the time, having completed a rare European Cup double and broken the Spanish stranglehold on the trophy, the Benfica team were expected to go on and establish themselves as masters of European football. With a young Eusébio driving the side, a period of prolonged greatness beckoned. It never came and Benfica have not tasted European glory again since that night in Amsterdam.

The Lisbon-based team had the chance to claim a European club treble in 1963 but were beaten at Wembley Stadium by Milan. The team didn't have to wait long for the next opportunity – a 1965 final against Internazionale – but again an Italian side had the better of them. Unbelievably, Benfica were back in London in 1968 for their fifth final in eight years. They were targeting a hat-trick of wins but instead went home nursing a trio of defeats, losing to George Best's Manchester United.

Benfica would have to wait until the 1980s for another stab at European glory. They played a UEFA Cup final in 1983 and a European Cup final in 1988. They lost both. Just two years after losing to PSV Eindhoven, they were within 90 minutes of Europe's biggest prize again. Reportedly, a retired Eusébio went to Guttmann's grave in an attempt to lift the curse. It didn't work. Again they lost. Again to Milan. Fast forward to 2013, when Benfica were in the Europa League final (the successor to the UEFA Cup). They played and lost to Chelsea. Undeterred, the Portuguese side returned in the Europa League decider in 2014. This time against Sevilla. No change in result though. Eight finals and eight defeats. 2062 can't come quick enough for Benfica.

FOOTBALL MOMENT

1997, I was at home, 17 years old, and it was Barcelona and Atlético Madrid. They were playing the second match of a quarter-final. In minute 8, Pantic scored for Atlético Madrid (score: 0–1); in minute 28, Pantic scored again (score: 0–2); in minute 31, Pantic scored a third goal (score: 0–3). I think it was his first hat-trick! In minute 47, Ronaldo scored for Barcelona (score: 1–3); in minute 51, Ronaldo scored again (score: 2–3). You expect Barcelona's third goal but suddenly, who scores in minute 52? Pantic! (Score: 2–4.) The incredible part is that I think he is the only football player who scored four goals in a match and lost the game. In minute 67 Figo scored for Barcelona (score: 3–4); in minute 72 Ronaldo scored again (score: 4–4); and in minute 82 Pizzi scored for Barcelona (score: 5–4). It was incredible.

Victor, Spain

13

French striking legend Just Fontaine holds the record for the most goals scored at a single World Cup tournament. In 1958, he found the back of the net an incredible 13 times, including hat-tricks against Paraguay and West Germany. Despite Fontaine's prolific goalscoring, France fell at the semi-final stage.

REVIE'S REGRETS

Believe it or not, Leeds United were an English footballing powerhouse in the 1960s and 1970s. Not many people liked them outside of Yorkshire, but they were still a force very much to be reckoned with. And to be fair to them, they didn't always come second, they just did it a lot.

Club manager Don Revie dragged Leeds to the first division in 1964 and for the next ten years they were one of Europe's best teams. They were English league champions twice, won two European Fairs Cups (the precursor to the UEFA Cup) and claimed one FA Cup, one League Cup and one FA Charity Shield (an annual game between the previous season's league and FA cup winners). Yet they could have won so much more. Between 1964 and 1975, the Yorkshire side fell at the last hurdle in major competitions a staggering ten times.

Under Revie, the Whites finished runners-up in the league an incredible five times, losing out on goal difference to Manchester United in 1964–1965, by six points to Liverpool in 1965–1966, by nine points to Everton in 1969–1970, by one point to Arsenal in 1970–1971 and by one point to the much unfancied Derby County in 1971–1972.

Cup competitions produced equal amounts of heartbreak. Leeds lost FA Cup finals in 1965, 1970 and 1973, the latter to Sunderland, a team playing in the Second Division. There were also defeats in two European Fairs Cup finals, to Dinamo Zagreb and Juventus, and one Cup Winners' Cup final, to Milan. The latter game was marred by accusations of match-fixing, with UEFA later banning the referee.

A change of manager wouldn't improve Leeds fortunes. Brian Clough was in and out in a flash, but that didn't stop him losing a FA Charity Shield against Liverpool. Jimmy Armfield did better, reinvigorating an ageing team and taking them to the 1975 European Cup final against Bayern Munich. Nevertheless, the Germans won 2–0.

BOUNCE-BACK BALLACK

Every player needs a bit of luck to win trophies. All the skill and spirit in the world can be rendered void if it isn't accompanied with a dash of fortune. German football legend Michael Ballack must wonder if he smashed a room full of mirrors as a child. He finished as a runner-up in major competitions a Kleenex-melting 12 times.

His career is littered with second-place finishes, but two years stand out in particular. In 2002, the German Bundesliga (the equivalent of the English Premier League) and the German League Cup (with Bayer Leverkusen) would go begging, and

Ballack would be suspended for a World Cup final that his side would lose. By 2008, the German was plying his trade for Premier League side Chelsea. The London team would finish second in the league and lose both a Champions League final and a League Cup final. In the same year, Ballack would captain Germany to the final of the European Championship, losing to Spain.

Three more second-place finishes in the Bundesliga can be added to the list (two with Bayer Leverkusen and one with Bayern Munich), as can a Premier League silver medal with Chelsea. However, he wasn't a complete stranger to glory, winning titles and cup medals in England and Germany, as well as plenty of individual awards, so he wasn't always the bridesmaid. Just quite a lot.

MARVELLOUS MALDINI

Paolo Maldini isn't a serial loser, he's a serial winner. It is testament to his ability that his career includes so many near misses and he's unlikely to reflect too much on the times he finished runner-up for the sole reason that he ended up first on so many more occasions. Still, 17 silver medals is an awful lot.

Maldini is Italian footballing aristocracy – son to Cesare, a football legend in his own right, and a rare one-club man. Joining as a youth player, he amassed a record-breaking 902 appearances for Milan, captaining the team for many seasons, in a club career that spanned almost 25 years. He also skippered the national team, racking up 126 caps over 14 years. He is considered one of the greatest defenders of all time.

He ended up on the losing side in a few big games though. With Milan, there was no cigar at the end of three Champions League finals, three Intercontinental/Club World finals, two Coppa Italia finals, three Supercoppa Italianas and one UEFA Super Cup final. He also came up just short in Serie A three times. In Azzurri blue, he would have to accept second place at the 1994 World Cup and Euro 2000.

Even in retirement the quest for medals goes on. In 2015, Maldini became the co-owner of new North American Soccer League club Miami FC. So far, no second-place finishes for Paolo's boys.

FOOTIE FACT

Paolo Maldini was the captain of Milan when they won the 2003 Champions League final in England. Forty years earlier his father, Cesare, did exactly the same thing – he led Milan to European Cup glory in England in the 1963 final.

GREAT FOOTBALLING RIVALRIES

. . . .

> *There are two great teams on Merseyside:*
> *Liverpool and Liverpool Reserves.*
> **BILL SHANKLY**

Where would football be without the bitter rivalries, the timeless feuds or the great grudges? It wouldn't be nearly as much fun. Club football is especially good at spite-filled showdowns. Lines are drawn, lifelong allegiances are sworn and the banter is never less than biting.

CLUB FOOTBALL'S FIERCEST FEUDS

ENGLAND   Liverpool v Manchester United

SPAIN   Barcelona v Real Madrid

ITALY   Roma v Lazio

GERMANY	Bayern Munich v Borussia Dortmund
HOLLAND	Ajax v Feyenoord
SCOTLAND	Celtic v Rangers
TURKEY	Fenerbahçe v Galatasaray
BRAZIL	Palmeiras v Corinthians
GREECE	Olympiakos v Panathinaikos
EGYPT	Al Ahly v Zamalek
ARGENTINA	Boca Juniors v River Plate

23

One-club man and Roma legend Francesco Totti is the first player to score in 23 consecutive seasons in Serie A, the Italian equivalent of the Premier League. Making his debut in 1992, the Giallorossi captain has found the back of the net in every campaign since, becoming the club's record goalscorer and second highest marksman of all time in the Italian top flight.

FOOTBALL MOMENT

Argentina in 2000. The two biggest clubs in the country, Boca Juniors and River Plate, were playing their second match in the quarter-finals of the Copa Libertadores. The first match had been won 2–1 by River Plate, so Boca needed two or more goals to go through. After six months of recovery from a very nasty knee injury, the main striker of the team, Martín Palermo, was back on the bench, and Boca's coach Carlos Bianchi had announced that he may let Palermo play for a few minutes. This statement brought all sorts of mockery from the rival coach, who said that if Bianchi let Palermo play, he would bring back Enzo Francescoli (former retired glory player of River).

With the match at 1–0 for Boca, Bianchi let Palermo in. Two minutes after that, there was a penalty for Boca, which Riquelme converted. And only a few minutes after that, Palermo, extremely slow and clumsy as his recovery was not full yet, received the ball in the area, turned around virtually in slow motion, and to the disbelief of his rivals, scored for his team. 3–0. The whole stadium exploded and the Boca fans began singing to River's coach, demanding he bring back Francescoli. And so did I, at home with my two best friends. Singing, yelling. For the victory against the rival, and for the return of our Titan.

Fernando, Argentina

International football is also littered with caustic conflicts. Argentina and Brazil have butted heads for a long time over Latin American supremacy; Holland and Germany have particularly spiky history when it comes to playing football; and more recently Russia and Ukraine have had to be kept apart on the pitch. The English like a good rivalry too.

ENGLAND VERSUS SCOTLAND

While a decline in the standard of Scottish football has dimmed the profile of this game in recent times, the intensity that surrounds it remains as fierce as ever. Asked who he would support at the 2010 World Cup, Scotland's Andy Murray replied 'anyone but England', which tells you all you need to know.

The first international match ever to be played was England against Scotland, with the inaugural showdown taking place in 1872. The final score was 0–0, with few fireworks to report, but all that would change. Over time, each team would hand out a shellacking or two to the other, but few were as fearful as the 9–3 victory inflicted by England in 1961, which reportedly helped the Scottish goalkeeper decide to emigrate to Australia.

However, revenge would be sweet for the Tartan Army. Fresh from their finest hour, Alf Ramsey's World Cup winners took on Scotland at the old Wembley in 1967. Full of swagger, England were massive favourites and seemingly certain of victory. But they were beaten 3–2 and the Scots claimed possibly their most famous triumph. Somewhat cheekily, they crowned themselves unofficial champions of the world.

Ten years later, England against Scotland made the headlines again, although the football had little to do with it. By this time, England were in the doldrums, having failed to reach an international tournament since 1970 (a run that would continue until 1980) and Scotland were enjoying a purple patch. It is hard to imagine that their supporters didn't take every opportunity to remind the English about it. Still, their celebrations after a 2–1 win in London remain infamous to this day. The Tartan Army invaded the pitch, tearing it up as they went and using the goalposts as monkey bars, eventually snapping one set in half.

In the wake of this match, England against Scotland became a marked game, with authorities ever more concerned over the likelihood of violence. In 1989, it disappeared from the international calendar, not to be seen for seven years. However, as the Madness song goes, you can't keep a good thing down and when the game did return, it was in some style.

England was hosting the 1996 European Championship and the team were drawn against Scotland in their group. The old rivalry was back on, the heat was turned back up again and the fans got a game to savour. The pivotal moment saw Scotland's captain Gary McAllister miss a penalty and England's Paul Gascoigne (better known as Gazza) head straight up the other end to put his team 2–0 up with one of the goals of the tournament. For a moment, the Three Lions had their supporters believing football was coming home.

FOOTIE FACT

Scotland have played at eight World Cups, but actually qualified for nine. Having qualified for the 1950 tournament in Sweden, the Scottish FA refused to let the team go because they weren't the British champions. Hubris 1, common sense 0.

ENGLAND VERSUS GERMANY

*Football is a simple game; 22 men chase a ball for
90 minutes and at the end the Germans win.*
GARY LINEKER

Germany is another of England's famous footballing foes.
England may have beaten the Tartan Army at Euro 96, but
they wouldn't get the best of another arch rival later in the
competition: English dreams were crushed mercilessly by
Germany in the semi-final – an all-too-familiar feeling for the
English.

So where did it all start to go wrong for England when it
came to playing Germany? The 4–2 victory over West Germany
in 1966 is a high point to which English football has never
returned. Things started to take a turn for the worse in the
blazing heat of Mexico in 1970. England were the reigning
world champions and, with arguably a stronger side, they were
confident of defending their crown. Progressing to the quarter-
finals, England were pitted against the West Germans once
again and, 2–0 up after 50 minutes, they looked on course to
record another victory. However, it was not to be: the stand-in
goalie Peter Bonetti made a massive blunder, striker Jeff Aston
missed an absolute sitter and the game finished 3–2 in the West
Germans' favour.

And so England's stupor began. It wasn't until 1982 that the
team returned to the World Cup and it wasn't until 1990 that
they got close to a final again. After a bad start, England found
some rhythm and squeaked through to the semi-finals, where

they faced a familiar foe. All England fans will know what happened next: a quite incredible game tipped one way and the other, West Germany scored, Lineker equalised, Gazza cried, it went to penalties and German ruthlessness won the day.

If that defeat left England fans heartbroken, then the result of the semi-final at Euro 96 inflicted some serious mental scars, not only with regard to playing the Germans but also taking penalties. Again, the game was a tight affair and, in front of their home fans, England looked to avenge that painful night in Turin. But it didn't happen: penalties decided the tie again, and again England came up short, with Gareth Southgate joining Chris Waddle and Stuart Pearce in England's penalty hall of shame. Not that they would be alone for long – many others would follow.

ENGLAND VERSUS ARGENTINA

One of the displays of abject penalty-taking by England that followed the losses in 1990 and 1996 was against Argentina in the 1998 World Cup. Paul Ince and David Batty would be ushered into the unfortunate pantheon of England players to mess up from 12 yards. The chance to avenge an infamous defeat was spurned.

Like the feud with Germany, England's beef with Argentina goes back to 1966. The events of a quarter-final game between the two sides sparked a fierce rivalry that continues to this day. England won 1–0 thanks to a Geoff Hurst goal, but it was the sending off of the Argentinian captain Antonio Rattín that would cause the bad blood. Reports vary regarding the reason for Rattín's dismissal, but, in the end, so furious was the player that he had to be escorted from the pitch by the police. The Argentinians were labelled animals, and the press and public at home were duly outraged.

They say that revenge is a dish best served cold – and it doesn't get much colder than, 20 years later, one of the most infamous incidents the World Cup has ever seen. Diego Maradona's 'Hand of God' in the quarter-final of the 1986 World Cup in Mexico has gone down in the tournament's history, and despite the fact that he scored one of the best goals ever seen at a World Cup later in the game, and that his imperious team would go on to lift the trophy, it was an act that few English fans have been able to forget or forgive. But for Argentinian fans simmering over the injustice of 1966, and the Falklands War in 1982, it didn't matter in the slightest. The English press got itself into an unholy funk, but for Argentina, karma had come calling and England were conquered when it mattered the most.

The 1998 World Cup in France offered England a chance to exorcise this particular demon, but David Beckham's red card, along with the inability of his teammates to muster a victory from 12 yards, meant that the Three Lions had to wait longer for some closure. The opportunity came again in 2002, this time at the World Cup co-hosted by Japan and South Korea, where the two sides faced each other at the group stage and, for once, England didn't pass it up. Beckham scored from the penalty spot, gaining redemption for the events of four years earlier, England won 1–0 and Argentina exited the tournament early.

FOOTIE FACT

In 1978, Sheffield United arranged to sign a 17-year-old Maradona for £200,000, but had to pull out of the deal because they couldn't afford it.

10

The first half of the Scottish league game between Motherwell and Dumbarton in 1954 was a record-breaking 45 minutes of football. When the referee blew his whistle, it wasn't just the players that needed a break. The fans had witnessed an incredible ten goals, with Motherwell going in 6–4 to the good. The second half failed to live up to the first. Still, the game finished 6–6.

THE DARK SIDE
OF THE BALL

· ·

*❝ I wasn't refereeing, I was acting as an umpire
in military manoeuvres. ❞*

KEN ASTON ON HIS EXPERIENCE AS THE REFEREE OF THE 1962 BATTLE OF SANTIAGO

The beautiful game; sometimes it isn't so beautiful. Sometimes
the handbags become properly argy-bargy. Sometimes football
games are like wars. Sometimes they start wars.

THE BATTLE OF SANTIAGO

The 1960s was a time of peace and love, but both these
sentiments were in very short supply during the match between
Chile and Italy at the 1962 World Cup. A metaphorical fire
had already been lit under the game – Chile, as hosts, had
struggled to prepare for the tournament following the Valdivia
earthquake and a couple of Italian journalists had mercilessly
laid into the state of the capital Santiago, making a song and
dance about some perceived inadequacies. The locals became so

incensed that the two hacks had to leave the country for their own safety. To no one's great surprise, as soon as the whistle was blown the game didn't take very long to explode: the first foul was committed after a matter of seconds, followed swiftly by a sending off after just 12 minutes. The culprit, the Italian Giorgio Ferrini, refused to go and had to be escorted from the pitch, kicking and screaming, by the police.

From then on in, the game slowly descended into violent farce with retaliation following retaliation. Mario David was the second and, unfathomably, the last man to get an early bath, for a flying kick to the head of Chile's Alexis Sánchez. In David's defence, Sánchez had not long before dropped him with a left hook. Sánchez wasn't finished either – he broke the nose of another Italian player later in the game. A football game did break out briefly, albeit with Italy having only nine men. Needless to say it was Chile that won. No wonder the English referee Ken Aston went on to invent the yellow and red cards.

THE BATTLE OF NUREMBERG

If the Battle of Nuremberg in 2006, featuring Holland and Portugal at the World Cup in Germany, teaches us one lesson, it's that football isn't very good at learning lessons. The advent of televised football and its growth into a global phenomenon has arguably made players a little more wary of committing out and out GBH on a football pitch – the Battle of Santiago was in some ways the end of an era – but the Dutch and Portuguese players contesting this Round-of-16 game seemed to undergo some collective brain freeze, kicking each other (and occasionally a ball) around the pitch for 90 bruising minutes.

Holland's Mark van Bommel set the tone after just two minutes, before teammate Khalid Boulahrouz well and truly ignited the blue touch paper with a murderous challenge on a young Cristiano Ronaldo, which put an end to the Portuguese's game. From there on in the tackles came thick and fast, most of which were late, high or both. By the time the final whistle went, it was a nine-a-side game whose Russian referee had managed to dish out 16 yellow cards in addition to the two red ones, which is a World Cup record.

FOOTIE FACT

Marco Materazzi, famously headbutted by Zinedine Zidane in the 2006 World Cup final, played a single season in the English Premier League. In just 27 appearances for Everton, he picked up three red cards and 12 yellows. That's some going.

THE FOOTBALL WAR

Did the World Cup qualifying matches between El Salvador and Honduras in 1969 start the Football War? Well, yes and no. Relations between the two countries were already at breaking point thanks to trade, land and immigration issues, but the three games between the two sides proved the tipping point.

In hindsight, the last thing that needed to happen was a large-scale display of nationalism. But, of course, it did and the results were predictably incendiary. The febrile atmosphere and violence that engulfed the ties was the spark that brought the two countries into open conflict. The decisive third game (held in neutral Mexico) – each side had won one match before that – hadn't even taken place before El Salvador broke off diplomatic relations with Honduras. Just over two weeks after they had booked their place at the World Cup, they had invaded their neighbours. The war lasted just 100 hours and El Salvador's World Cup only three matches, in which they failed to bother the scoresheet once.

548

During his 19-year club career, most of it spent at Italian side Inter Milan, Javier Zanetti earned a reputation as one of the game's most respected players. Captaining the Milan side for much of that time, the Argentinian international racked up 615 league appearances for the club between 1995 and 2014. Remarkably, he didn't get a red card until his 548th game. There would not be another.

THE MARK OF A (FOOTBALLING) MAN

Violence in football isn't always a team affair. Sometimes it can be a solo act. The history of the game is littered with the boneheaded actions of individual players, whether committed against opponents, teammates, officials or fans. But there are those that have left a bigger mark than others.

FLIPPING THE BIRDS

One of the most infamous acts of on-field thuggery in the modern game didn't happen on the pitch at all. For all his sublime skill and winners' medals, Eric Cantona is remembered by many for the flying kung-fu attack he carried out on a nasty Crystal Palace fan in 1995. The supporter reportedly hurled a missile and racist abuse at the Manchester United number seven, who responded by launching himself feet first into the crowd, with fists whirling, to deal with his tormentor.

While the Frenchman received some sympathy from within the game, the authorities were anything but understanding. Cantona was initially handed a two-week jail sentence, which was eventually reduced to 120 hours of community service, and the FA banned him for nine months and fined him £20,000. For good measure, the French Football Federation stripped him of the captaincy of the national side and chucked him out of the team. For Cantona, it was a heavy price to pay for losing his famously fiery temper, but there was a silver lining of sorts: the game did get one of its best quotes of all time:

> *When the seagulls follow the trawler, it's because they think sardines will be thrown into the sea. Thank you very much.*
> **ERIC CANTONA'S CRYPTIC RESPONSE TO HIS PUNISHMENT**

QUICK TO BITE

When you hear a commentator say that a player is quick to bite, 99 times of 100 he means that the person in question has a short temper and can be easily riled. But what about that other time? That time is Luis Suárez.

In a game deflated by a glut of hyperbole, it is fair to say that the Uruguayan striker is a genuine footballing genius. It's just a shame that he makes the headlines too often for the wrong reasons. He has used his hands, his mouth and, yes, his teeth to stain his reputation. That Suárez bit an Italian defender during a game at the 2014 World Cup didn't come as a massive surprise: he had form in this area. In 2013, while playing for Liverpool, he sunk his gnashers into a Chelsea defender. This followed an incident in 2010 when he chowed down on an opponent's shoulder while captaining Dutch side Ajax. FIFA banned the player for nine months, outdoing both the English and Dutch FAs, which dished out ten- and eight-match bans respectively.

OVER KEANE

No look at football's famous sinners is complete without mention of Roy Keane. It's fair to say that the red mist descended upon him a few times. The act of savagery for which he is most notorious is the tackle on Alf-Inge Haaland that all but ended the Norwegian's career. There was plenty of backstory to the knee-high tackle but the challenge itself has had a much longer life span. The Republic of Ireland player initially only received the regulation three-match ban, but mention of the tackle, and in particular its premeditated nature, in his autobiography the following year brought an extra five-match ban and a fine of £150,000. Needless to say, to this day the foul still remains a talking point when discussing the Red Devil legend's career.

FOOTIE FACT

'The Sh*t Hits the Fan' – newspaper headline after Eric Cantona's infamous attack on a Crystal Palace supporter in 1995.

OFF FOR AN EARLY BATH

Today it's something of a surprise if a game doesn't feature a flurry of yellow cards and the odd red one. But there was a time when players had to commit something bordering on GBH for the referee to reach into his pocket. There was even a time when there were no cards at all.

Red and yellow cards were invented by referee Ken Aston in the 1960s and were based, in a wonderfully British way, on traffic lights. They were first used at a World Cup in 1970 and in domestic football in 1976. Naturally, players have been setting disciplinary milestones ever since.

- First red card: Carlos Caszely, Chile v West Germany, 1974

- First football league red card: David Wagstaffe, Blackburn Rovers v Leyton Orient, 1976

- First red card in an FA Cup final: Kevin Moran, Manchester United v Everton, 1985

- Quickest red card at a World Cup: 1 minute, José Batista, Uruguay v Scotland, 1986

- First England red card at a World Cup: Ray Wilkins, England v Morocco, 1986

- First red card in a World Cup final: Pedro Monzón, Argentina v West Germany, 1990

- First red card in the Premier League: Tony Cascarino, Chelsea v Leeds, 1993

- First World Cup red card on a player's birthday: Gianfranco Zola, Italy v Nigeria, 1994

- First England red card at Wembley: Paul Scholes, England v Sweden, 1999

- First red card at the new Wembley: Matthew Gill, Exeter v Morecambe, 2007

FOOTBALL MOMENT

It is hard to choose between Germany versus the Netherlands in 1988 and Spain versus the Netherlands in 2014. Winning against Germany in the semi-final of Euro 1988 was probably more important to me and most Dutch people than winning the title by beating Russia in the final. It was finally revenge for 1974 and I still remember the celebrations in my student town, Groningen, where people were climbing on and driving buses to celebrate the victory after Van Basten's winning goal. But I still go for the 5-1 victory against world champions Spain during the World Cup in Brazil. Expectations before the tournament were low; we were almost 2-0 down, but then the amazing equaliser from "Flying Dutchman" Van Persie. That changed everything. The second half of that match was the best I have ever seen in a stadium, with fantastic goals from Robben; we could have scored eight. So although the joy of beating Germany was probably even higher, from a football point of view, witnessing the Dutch national team crushing Spain was better.

Marko, the Netherlands

Serious sport has nothing to do with fair play. It is bound up with hatred, jealousy, boastfulness, disregard of all rules and sadistic pleasure in witnessing violence: in other words it is war minus the shooting.

GEORGE ORWELL

FOOTBALL SCANDALS

·······································

> *Professional football is something like war.*
> *Whoever behaves too properly is lost.*
>
> **DUTCH FOOTBALL VISIONARY RINUS MICHELS**

Football is big business these days. Its soul is fast becoming lost in the pursuit of more customers and income rather than more fans and support. It's a breeding ground for corruption. But football scandals aren't a new phenomenon; they're almost as old as the game itself. The desire to win and the excess that comes with success make people do crazy, stupid things, and the history of the game is littered with eye-boggling examples.

ITALIAN BLUES

You could be forgiven for thinking Italy fans welcome a scandal. Italian football was rocked by big ones in 1980, 2006 and 2012, and in the major international tournaments that followed the national team played some of the most successful football of the modern era. Controversy it seems is a strong motivator for the Azzurri.

TOTONERO

The first major match-fixing scandal to hit Italian football in the modern era was the Totonero affair in 1980. There is an old-fashioned feel to the circumstances surrounding this bad-betting-borne balls up, a wistful dash of amateurism, that shows just how the game has changed since.

At the heart of the scandal that would engulf heavyweight clubs and over 30 officials and players was a pair of shopkeepers from Rome. The story goes that the duo were embroiled in efforts to rig games by bribing players but, with the fixing not going to plan, had found themselves hopelessly in debt. In a ludicrous attempt to raise the money and pay off their creditors, they had the chutzpah to try to blackmail the Italian Football Federation. It didn't work and the lid was lifted on a whole lot of corruption.

The punishment for those involved was stiff and included demotions, point deductions and bans. Milan and Lazio were relegated to the second tier, Liga B, and Serie A sides Bologna and Perugia were docked points. One of the players singled out was Serie A golden boy Paolo Rossi, who was one of the most expensive footballers in the world at the time. He was banned for three years, which meant that Italy would be without one of their best striking hopes for the 1982 World Cup.

However, redemption would come Rossi's way, when his ban was reduced to one year on appeal. Conveniently this meant he was free to play for the Italian national team in Spain. And what an impact he had. After a slow start, the Perugia striker found his groove, scoring six goals to earn the competition's Golden Boot and propel Italy to World Cup glory.

CALCIOPOLI

Match-fixing reared its ugly head in Italy again in 1986 (Totonero II), but it wasn't until 2006 that the country had to stomach another grand football scandal. And this one is perhaps the largest scandal of its type that the sport has ever seen.

The principal protagonists were Juventus general managers Luciano Moggi and Antonio Giraudi. Undone by police wiretaps, the two were placed at the centre of a conspiracy to fix matches in Serie A that involved no less than 50 club officials, national football authority executives and referees. The level of corruption shook Italian football to its very core and sent shockwaves through the global game.

The affair broke not long before the World Cup, which meant Italian football approached the tournament mired in muck and thoroughly distracted; many of the national team's best players belonged to the clubs at the heart of the scandal. The fallout was extraordinary – Juventus were stripped of two Serie A championships, relegated to Serie B and barred from the Champions League; Lazio were stopped from playing in the UEFA Cup; Fiorentina were chucked out of the Champions League; and Milan and Reggina were given hefty points deductions.

Yet these punishments weren't meted out until after the World Cup. First, the Azzurri had to play in Germany. And as in 1982, they found scandal no impediment to success. Italy saw off the effervescent hosts in a scintillating semi-final and a Henry-and-Zidane-fired France in the final to claim their fourth title on a blistering night in Berlin.

SCOMMESSOPOLI

The Scommessopoli match-fixing scandal in 2012 wasn't as high profile as the Calciopoli affair but it hit Italian football just as hard, perhaps even harder. The punch behind this betting scandal was its sheer scale – it involved a whopping 21 football clubs. Most of them were lower-league teams but the corruption was vast.

Arrests came thick and fast, with 19 alleged conspirators detained by Italian police, including Lazio captain Stefano Mauri. The *carabinieri* also turned up at national team's Coverciano training base to question Domenico Criscito. The defender was subsequently dropped from the Italy squad. Such was the shame that Italian football had been stained by another huge match-fixing scandal, and just six years after the last one, that the prime minister and national manager of the time Mario Monti and Cesare Prandelli went to UEFA and offered to withdraw Italy from Euro 2012.

Yet the suits in Nyon declined and Italy went to the tournament being hosted by Ukraine and Poland. They navigated a tricky group stage, before swatting aside England in the quarters and ousting one of the favourites Germany in the semis. However, unlike in 1982 and 2006, the Italians wouldn't turn crushing corruption into ultimate victory. A weary and injury hit Azzurri succumbed to a majestic Spain in the final. Still, Italy had carried dishonour with a singular elegance once again.

FOOTBALL MOMENT

Lazio v Roma, 1998. The year before, Roma had lost four derbies out of four. Roma scored the first goal. It seemed the end of the nightmare. But Lazio's Roberto Mancini equalized at the end of the first half. Second half: Mancini again and a Salas penalty for SS Lazio, and second yellow card for a Roma defender. 3–1 to Lazio, and Roma a man down. Roma had never lost five consecutive derbies. It would be a humiliation impossible to forget. 15 minutes to go: Di Francesco scored, 3–2. When all hope was lost, 22-year-old Francesco Totti scored his first goal in a derby. But it was not over: 93rd minute: a ball in the box and Roma scored. 4–3, but disallowed! All the newspapers the next day would call that offside 'a mistake'. Final score 3–3. Never so many emotions in 95 minutes.

Giovanni, Italy

58

The reputation and car of Arsenal and England captain Tony Adams suffered a sizeable dent in May 1990 when he crashed his Ford Sierra into a wall while being four times over the legal drink-driving limit. He served 58 days in prison as a result. When the Gunners' skipper retired, he set up Sporting Chance, a charity to aid sportsmen and women suffering from addiction.

THE WORLD CUP OF FRAUD

Sports scandals don't come any bigger than those that involve world governing bodies, and football does things bigger than anyone else. And so it proved on 3 December 2015 when, in the early hours of the morning, the roof fell in on FIFA.

When the Swiss authorities mounted their dawn raid on the luxury Baur au Lac hotel, arresting FIFA executives (including two of its vice presidents), the organisation that was suspected of being riddled with corruption was shown to be just that.

The arrests were the result of a three-year investigation by US authorities, including the FBI and the Internal Revenue Service, which indicted the FIFA officials for money laundering, racketeering and wire fraud offences, among other crimes. It was alleged that officials had taken bribes and kickbacks worth more than $150 million from US and South American sports marketing executives. The Internal Revenue Service called it the 'World Cup of fraud'.

A CURIOUS QATAR AND A RUM RUSSIA

When Sepp Blatter opened the envelope to reveal the winner of the competition to host the 2022 World Cup and held aloft the name of Qatar, the jaws of the football world hit the floor. A tiny Middle Eastern state with no footballing history, that had never qualified for a World Cup, that boasts summer temperatures in excess of 50 degrees Celsius, where alcohol and drunkenness are banned and whose laws deem homosexuality illegal, had triumphed over the likes of Australia, Japan, the USA and South Korea.

Such was the astonishment and subsequent consideration given to the Qatar bid win that Russia's victory in capturing the 2018 tournament was initially afforded little attention. However, as the dust settled, eyebrows were also raised over this decision.

Somewhat admirably, FIFA didn't bury its head in the sand. In the wake of the accusations following the controversial decisions, the organisation launched an inquiry, headed by independent American lawyer Michael Garcia. Somewhat less admirably, it completely ignored the inquiry's findings. Garcia said that he had found 'serious and wide-ranging issues' with the bidding and selection of the two host nations. 'Oh no there weren't,' said the official summary released by FIFA's Ethics Committee. Garcia resigned in protest but, while FIFA's critics had more fuel to fire their suspicions, nothing changed. However, little did FIFA know that the countdown had begun to the dawn raid in Zurich, and that was thanks largely to one man: Chuck Blazer.

Charles 'Chuck' Blazer, a former General Secretary of the Confederation of North, Central American and Caribbean Association Football (CONCACAF), was one of the main reasons FIFA luminaries such as Vice Presidents Jeffrey Webb and Eugenio Figueredo never got to breakfast on 3 December 2015. Facing multiple charges of bribery, tax evasion and money laundering, he turned informer for the FBI.

STEADFAST SEPP AND IMPECCABLE INFANTINO

One FIFA man who didn't feel the long arm of the Swiss law in December 2015 was the organisation's leader, Sepp Blatter. Yet there was no stopping his downfall. Later in December 2015, FIFA's Ethics Committee issued him with an eight-year ban for his involvement in a case that would also see UEFA lose its commander-in-chief, Michel Platini.

Blatter is still out there fighting his corner, but he did eventually leave the FIFA building. However, the world's best football teams will still criss-cross Russia in 2018 to fight it out for the game's ultimate honour, and yes, the competition will still plot a course for Qatar in 2022. But at least the players won't have to endure skin-melting temperatures, because the tournament has been shifted to the winter for the first time in its history. Never mind the havoc it will wreak on domestic competitions in Europe.

So, who has come to the rescue of FIFA? Did the organisation elect an independent individual unconnected with the scandal? No, of course they didn't. They chose UEFA Secretary General Gianni Infantino, who was almost immediately accused of involvement with indicted figures and FIFA corruption scandals. *Plus ça change*, you may think. But, what's that? Is it the FIFA Ethics Committee to the rescue? Yes, it is! They cleared Gianni of any wrongdoing in the summer of 2016.

DRUGGED-UP DIEGO

It should have been obvious. Perhaps it was. Argentina were playing Greece in their opening game at the 1994 World Cup and Diego Maradona scored a goal to seal the points for La Albiceleste. The side's captain and talisman embarked on what can only be called an extremely exuberant celebration. He was wild, screaming into camera, eyes bulging from his head. Yes, it was pretty clear.

That Maradona had got to the tournament was a minor miracle. In the early 1990s, his star was waning and his off-field behaviour was getting him into more and more trouble. Quite literally, he was looking less and less like a footballer.

In 1991, while playing in Italy for Napoli, he tested positive for cocaine. He was banned for 15 months by FIFA and fled the country before he could face criminal charges. In his absence, he was fined and given a suspended prison sentence. Back in Argentina, after a year in Spain at Sevilla, he was caught with half a kilogram of cocaine but somehow avoided jail. In 1993, he joined local side Newell's Old Boys but his failure to make training meant that he made only five appearances before leaving. In early 1994, he shot at journalists with an airgun outside his home in Buenos Aires.

So it was all looking pretty bleak for Maradona and one last World Cup final appearance seemed a pipe dream. However, he wasn't to be denied his dream and made a huge effort to make it in to the Argentina team for the tournament in the USA. Too much effort as it turned out. Somewhat unsurprisingly, after the game against Greece, Diego was called in for a routine drugs test. It came back positive for a whole load of the banned stimulant ephedrine – five variants to be precise.

Ephedrine is taken by allergy and asthma sufferers and is also used as a weight-loss aid. Maradona claimed he had taken it for a cold. FIFA didn't believe him, chucked him of the World Cup and banned him for 15 months. The scandal knocked the wind out of Argentina's sails and they didn't make it past the first knockout round.

> **❝** *Roy Keane's on 50 grand a week. So was I till the police found my printing machine.* **❞**
>
> **FORMER WELSH AND MANCHESTER UNITED MIDFIELDER MICKEY THOMAS, WHO WAS JAILED FOR 18 MONTHS IN 1993 FOR PASSING ON FORGED BANKNOTES TO TEAMMATES**

THE FLIGHT OF THE CONDOR

Group 3 of the South American zone of qualification for the 1990 World Cup was on a knife edge. And it would be something sharp that decided who topped the three-team league and went to the tournament in Italy. Except it wasn't any kind of sublime shooting skills or an eagle-eyed piece of refereeing. It was something quite literal instead.

Chile turned up at the Maracanã on 3 September 1989 knowing that a draw against home team Brazil would be enough to see them through at the expense of their opponents, courtesy of a better goal difference. Brazil had to win to ensure their qualification and continue their uninterrupted attendance at the World Cup.

Brazil went ahead in the 49th minute and qualification was within reach. However, midway through the second half, a firework was thrown on to the pitch and Chilean goalkeeper Roberto Rojas, nicknamed the Condor, fell to the ground. By the time the television cameras picked him up, there was blood streaming from his head. Rojas was carried off and the game was abandoned.

The repercussions would have been serious for Brazil, with disqualification a real possibility. Yet luckily for them, a photographer had captured the exact moment the firework had hit the ground: it was metres away from Rojas. Challenged on the matter, the goalkeeper admitted that he had hidden a razor blade in his glove for such an eventuality. Rojas was given a lifetime ban and Chile were banned from the 1994 World Cup.

ALSO BANNED FROM THE WORLD CUP:

SEX

Bans on players having sex at major tournaments for the benefit of their game are pretty common, but the one imposed by Brazil manager Luiz Felipe Scolari at the 2002 World Cup in Japan and South Korea is particularly noteworthy. He outlawed any nookie for 40 days, from the day the players turned up to the training camp to the day they lifted the trophy. Libidinous star striker Ronaldo was not impressed and recalled that his memories of the tournament would always include that of an ache down below. It can't have been that bad because nine months after the tournament, a Japanese waitress gave birth to his child.

WAGS

The wives and girlfriends of the England players had created quite a stir at the 2006 World Cup. Their antics in the German spa town of Baden-Baden had led to a paparazzi frenzy that the players admitted some time later had affected their concentration. So four years on, the England manager Fabio Capello made sure there wouldn't be a repeat and imposed a curfew that allowed players to see their loved ones only for a few hours after each game. Not that it made much difference to the team's play. After a stuttering performance in the group stage, the Three Lions were destroyed by Germany in the first knockout stage.

LIVE BROADCASTS

North Korean leader Kim Jong-il – he who was born under a double rainbow, could control the weather and didn't defecate – banned live broadcasts of the side's games at the 2010 World Cup in South Africa. He obviously wasn't optimistic about their chances. Instead, domestic fans would get heavily edited highlights. Supporters may have got to see a fair bit of the first game against Brazil despite the 2–1 loss, but the highlights of the next match must have been very short – North Korea lost 7–0 to Portugal. Those of the last game against Ivory Coast (3–0) probably weren't much longer.

NICOLAS ANELKA

France has a tendency to be either very good or very bad at international tournaments. And the very bad is usually spectacularly so, with a bruising lack of *bon accord* between players and management a recurring theme. The 2010 World Cup was one of these times. Tension had been building and at half-time in their game against Mexico, striker Nicolas Anelka, having been criticised for his performance, lost his rag with the manager Raymond Domenech. He sent the air in the Blues changing room, well, blue. France went on to lose the match. Other players would rebel but Anelka was the main target of the ire that followed. The suits at the French Football Federation had a tantrum and senior politicians jumped quickly on the bandwagon. Anelka was handed an 18-game ban and waved *au revoir* to his international career.

ROY KEANE

During his illustrious and often infamous career Roy Keane was never anything less than forthright in his views and this was the case when he travelled to the 2002 World Cup with the Republic of Ireland. To be fair, he had a good reason for his World Cup-ending outburst. While the players flew economy to the tournament, the Football Association of Ireland officials lived it up in first class and when they all arrived, the training pitch was a mess and lots of gear was missing. Captain Keane was not a happy man and an unhappy Roy is a very dangerous thing. When he finally blew his lid at manager Mick McCarthy, it was some explosion. He unleashed an expletive-ridden tirade that ended with the captain telling his boss to 'stick it up your bollocks'. Keane was duly sent home from the tournament.

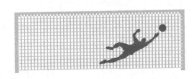

AN AGE-OLD PROBLEM

You have to go back to 1990 to find the last World Cup that Central American football heavyweights Mexico didn't qualify for. And it wasn't because they didn't cut the mustard in qualification; they were never given the chance because they were banned.

Two years previously, the Mexico under-20 team played in a tournament for teams belonging to the Confederation of North, Central American and Caribbean Association Football (CONCACAF) to determine who would qualify for the 1989 World Youth Championships in Saudi Arabia. The Mexicans topped their first round group and in the final group came second to Costa Rica. Both went through and would play in the Middle East the next year.

However, a Mexican journalist unearthed evidence in a football yearbook that some of the Mexican players were telling fibs about their ages. The story hit the headlines but the national football authorities pulled a collective I-don't-know-what-you're-talking-about face and denied it. Yet a subsequent investigation found four players to be overage, including captain Aurelio Rivera, who was four years over the age limit when he played.

Mexico were chucked out of the World Youth Championships – their desert dreams turned to dust – and replaced by the USA. Officials were given lifetime bans and the senior team was barred from international competitions for two years. This meant that there would be no Mexico at the 1988 Olympic Games or the 1990 World Cup.

MATCH FIT

In the run to the final of the 1998 World Cup, any team playing reigning champions Brazil had good reason to be fearful. That reason was called Ronaldo. Already a veteran of the 1994 World Cup winning squad, he had spent the intervening time announcing his immense talent to the world. There was no doubt that he would be another Brazilian football great. Yet in the final itself, France must have been a little less daunted.

When the team sheets were announced a few hours before the game there was a notable name missing: Ronaldo. The world was stunned and confusion reigned. Then with 40 minutes to kick-off his name reappeared. Cue even greater confusion. What was going on? Ronaldo came on to the pitch and started the game but the player that had mesmerised crowds, scoring four goals in the tournament, was there in form only. A ghost, he was all but invisible and the game passed him by like he wasn't there. Brazil slumped and the hosts won 3–0.

Everyone wanted to know what had happened. Ronaldo had suffered a convulsive fit. It was short but violent and had unnerved and upset his teammates. He had fallen unconscious for a few minutes and was taken to hospital, but tests found nothing untoward. So, having been given the all clear, Ronaldo returned to the squad and insisted he should play. And he did with catastrophic results for the team – their then heaviest World Cup defeat.

Speculation continues to this day as to what caused the seizure and why he was allowed to play. Conspiracy theorists claim a nervous breakdown, an allergic reaction to an injection of Xylocaine and sabotage by the French, while a teammate at the time claimed sponsors Nike had pressurised Brazil into playing their most marketable asset. Even more fanciful was a suggestion that there was no fit at all, but Ronaldo had simply been at odds with his teammates who had been bribed to throw the game.

As ever, the truth, about why he played at least, is much more mundane. Brazil team manager Mário Zagallo explained, 'If I didn't put Ronaldo on and then Brazil lost 3–0, people would say, "Zagallo is stubborn, he had to put him on, Ronaldo was the best player in the world."' The team doctor was even more frank, 'Imagine if I stopped him playing and Brazil lost. At that moment I'd have to go and live on the North Pole.'

Still, speaking in 2014, the striker himself breathed new life into the scandal by responding to a question about what had happened with: 'Was it pressure or nerves? It could be.'

NOTHING TO SEE HERE

> *I used to go missing a lot... Miss Canada,*
> *Miss United Kingdom, Miss World.*
> **GEORGE BEST**

Sometimes it's what doesn't happen that has a bigger impact than what does. Whether it's goals that were incorrectly given or ruled out, or gifted players walking away prematurely from the game, football is full of what-ifs and parallel universes. Technology is gradually helping to reduce the impact of controversy on the pitch, but perhaps we shouldn't try too hard. After all, it's the unpredictability of human nature and human fallibility that adds so much colour to the game and makes it so engrossing.

FIVE FAMOUS GOALS THAT WEREN'T

❶ PAUL SCHOLES V PORTO, CHAMPIONS LEAGUE 2004 ROUND OF 16

The assistant referee in this game changed football history. His excruciating error sent the game spinning off into an alternative universe. Manchester United were heading for victory that a close-range Scholes strike seemed to rubber-stamp. But the goal was ruled out for offside. Replays showed Scholes to be clearly onside. Porto would score, go through and go on to win the tournament. Their manager? One José Mourinho. Just think what would have happened if the officials got the decision right. No Special One and no jobs at Chelsea, Internazionale, Real Madrid and Manchester United. Football could have been very different.

② PEDRO MENDES V MANCHESTER UNITED, ENGLISH PREMIER LEAGUE 2005

Mendes' career at Tottenham Hotspur was far from memorable, but his time playing for the Lilywhites will never be forgotten because of this goal. In the dying minutes of the game against the then serial champions, the Red Devils' keeper Roy Carroll takes a free-kick some 35-40 yards from his goal. He fluffs it and Tottenham surge forward. As Carroll is furiously backpedalling, Mendes launches an audacious lob from just inside the United half. The keeper gets back and claims the ball but drops it over the line. More than a metre over the line. Inexplicably, the referee and his assistant don't give it.

③ KEVIN KEEGAN V MANCHESTER UNITED, ENGLISH FIRST DIVISION 1981

If there were a prize for the most pedantic refereeing decision in history, this would surely win it. England striker and double European player of the year Keegan scores what would probably have been the goal of the season. What the Saints striker does is simply incredible – with no shot seemingly on, he produces an astonishing piece of acrobatics, launching into a flying volley to connect with a ball that is going behind him, sending it roaring into the back of the net. However, an absurdly fussy piece of refereeing denied him any accolades. The man in black deemed that Saints' other forward Armstrong had been offside. He was nowhere near Keegan, never touched the ball and wasn't interfering with play. But rules were rules.

④ CRISTIANO RONALDO V SPAIN, 2010 INTERNATIONAL FRIENDLY

Ronaldo regularly divides opinion – he is clearly a footballing great, but the size of his ego rubs some people up the wrong way. However, love him or loathe him, it's hard not to feel sorry for him here. Portugal are playing old foes Spain, who are dominating world football. A Portuguese win would be huge. Captain Cristiano is on fire. Collecting the ball 25 yards out, he leads the Spanish defence a merry dance before executing a perfect chip from just outside the six-yard box to beat the goalkeeper. The ball is heading in and this Iberian derby will have one of its greatest goals. Except just as it is about to cross the line, Ronaldo's teammate Nani heads it. From an offside position. No goal. An apoplectic skipper doesn't hold back.

⑤ FRANK LAMPARD V GERMANY, 2010 WORLD CUP ROUND OF 16

This goal-that-wasn't changed football forever. There is nothing particularly unusual about it – the England midfielder smashes a shot against the bar, it drops a metre or so behind the line, the referees don't give it, Lampard and his teammates remonstrate loudly and the game carries on – but it was arguably the straw that broke the camel's back. Goal-line video technology would make an appearance not too long after. Did the decision alter the outcome of the game? Germany were 2-1 up at the time, so it would have been an equaliser. Could England have turned it around or would Germany have continued to dominate and still have thrashed the Three Lions? Probably the latter but you never know.

5

The league match between Crystal Palace and Brighton & Hove Albion in March 1989 featured an amazing five penalties. The referee awarded them in the space of just 27 minutes. The Eagles missed three of their four spot kicks, while the Seagulls scored their only penalty. Nevertheless, the Londoners still won 2–1.

OVER AND OUT: GOAL-LINE TECHNOLOGY

There's nothing like a volte-face from the game's highest-ranking administrator to underline just how disconnected ruling bodies are from their sport. Despite a growing number of goals-that-weren't in major matches, including those at its showpiece tournaments, FIFA and its all-powerful leader, Sepp Blatter, were as supportive of goal-line technology as a Manchester United fan would be of Liverpool Football Club. UEFA big cheese Michel Platini was even more dismissive of the concept.

But despite FIFA and UEFA, progress would not be stopped. Was it Frank Lampard's ghost strike against Germany at the 2010 World Cup? Was it the successful adoption of the technology by other competitions that showed just how deep administrators had their heads in the sand? Who knows? But one day, all of a sudden Blatter became goal-line technology's number one fan. The equipment would be used at the next World Cup in Brazil.

Despite Ukraine suffering an England-style injustice at Euro 2012 (against the Three Lions no less), Platini would take longer to relent. But he too eventually gave way, although he wouldn't be in power to see the technology used for the first time in major UEFA competitions. The equipment made its debut in the 2016 Champions League and Europa League at the competitions' finals and in the European Championship at the 2016 tournament in France.

FOOTIE FACT

The first goal to be given using goal-line technology in the English Premier League was scored by Manchester City striker Edin Džeko against Cardiff in January 2014.

THE APPEARANCE OF VANISHING SPRAY

Every Brazilian wants to forget the 2014 World Cup, right? Wrong. There is at least one man that looks back fondly on the tournament – the highlight of which was the home nation receiving a 7–1 semi-final mauling at the hands of Germany. His name is Heine Allemagne.

The tournament wrote Allemagne's name large in world football yet few fans would have known it had they heard it. What Heine did was to invent the vanishing spray and solve the age-old problem of the moving wall. In the tournament's opening game, hundreds of millions of people from around the world witnessed his mission-accomplished moment.

Vanishing spray is simple yet revolutionary. If one team wins a free kick near but not in their opponent's penalty area, the other team, in order to defend their goal, usually forms a wall, comprising two or more players. The wall must be ten yards from the ball. Keeping the wall this distance away was always a problem because players in the wall would try to shorten the distance to make it harder for the taker of the free kick to score. Allemagne brought this sneakiness to an end.

Watching a game as an unemployed man in 2000, it struck the football-mad Brazilian just how angry people on and off the field became when players tried to bring walls closer than ten yards. He wanted to do something about it and he had the perfect solution: a temporary white line marked out on the pitch that would ensure that players in the wall remained the right distance from the ball.

After demonstrating his idea with some shaving foam to an excited household, he prepared some notes and went to a local cosmetics company to work out a formula. This was the beginning of a 14-year journey that would culminate in the moment in the first half of the Brazil–Croatia game in São Paolo when Japanese referee Yuichi Nishimura awarded a free kick to the hosts and reached for a can of vanishing spray.

Yes, Germany's rout of Brazil in the semi-finals would make the tournament memorable for a very different reason, but perhaps with a surname like that (Allemagne is the French word for Germany), Germany was always going to play some role in the inventor's greatest moment.

FOOTIE FACT

The first goal to be given using goal-line technology at the World Cup was scored by French forward Karim Benzema against Honduras in June 2014.

FAMOUS FOOTBALL VANISHING ACTS

WEMBLEY TONI

There once was a time when beating England carried significant cachet. Those that scored in the process of doing so had considerable fame bestowed upon them. One such recipient was Anton 'Toni' Fritsch. On the evening of 20 October 1965, Austria became only the third continental team to beat England at Wembley, with the Rapid Vienna striker Fritsch scoring twice in a 3–2 victory against a side managed by Sir Alf Ramsey that would go on to win the World Cup the following year. History was made and a life long nickname of Wembley Toni conferred. Yet Fritsch would leave another profound mark on the world of sport. Six years later, at the age of just 26, he swapped the round ball for an egg-shaped one, signing as a place kicker for the Dallas Cowboys, an American football team. In 1972, he kicked a record number of field goals and was part of the side that won the Super Bowl. He would play for the San Diego Chargers, the Houston Oilers, the New Orleans Saints and the Houston Gamblers before returning to Vienna.

ROBIN FRIDAY

Robin Friday is probably the greatest footballer you've never heard of. His career was a blink-and-you'll-miss-it affair – it lasted less than four years and involved just two distinctly unglamorous professional teams, Reading and Cardiff City. Yet in his pomp those that saw Friday play readily compared him to the likes of Pelé and Johan Cruyff – outrageously skilled, he scored extraordinary goals for fun and famously tormented England World Cup-winning captain Bobby Moore. Reading fans voted him the club's player of the century. Why did he walk away from the beautiful game in 1977 aged just 26 having never played for a top-flight team? Well, sports journalist Paolo Hewitt's description of the man should tell you all you need to know: 'If George Best was football's first pop star, Robin was the game's first rock star.' A handful on the pitch, he was just as unpredictable off it, with an appetite for excess that would have given Belfast's famous footballing son pause for thought. He died of a suspected heroin overdose just 12 years later. His decision to retire so early is one of football's greatest losses.

MATTHIAS SINDELAR

Imagine if one day there was suddenly no more Messi or Ronaldo. Admittedly, Austria's greatest ever football player and captain of the revolutionary Wunderteam of the 1930s was much nearer retirement, but that moment came all the same.

Like Lionel and Cristiano, the Austria Vienna centre forward was one of best players on the planet at the time, his cerebral skills helping his club and the national side enjoy a period of glory that neither have ever experienced again. Both teams adhered to the Scottish style of quick passing and possession-based football, a philosophy that would instruct the famous Hungarian side of the 1950s, the Cruyff-driven Total Football of the 1970s and the world-conquering Barcelona and Spain teams of Guardiola and Del Bosque.

By 1939, the career of Der Papierene (Paper Man), a nod to his willowy frame, was coming to an end. He would have one last game for the Wunderteam, a match against Germany to mark the Anschluss. A liberal minded man, Sindelar refused to be a show pony for his country's new overlords. A goal and an assist from the striker earned Austria an unexpected 2–0 victory; he celebrated enthusiastically in front of the Nazi top brass in attendance. There would be no more international football for Unsere Burschen's golden boy; he wasn't interested in representing Germany.

Less than a year later, he was found dead in his flat in Vienna. The cause of death was officially recorded as accidental – carbon monoxide poisoning as a result of a faulty heater – and there is little evidence to suggest otherwise. But conspiracy theories abounded, with suicide and state-sponsored murder among the stories put forward. Whatever happened, Austria and the world lost one of its finest footballing talents that day.

FOOTBALL MOMENT

My best football moment is the 1994 world cup final between Brazil and Italy in the USA. I am a big fan of Brazil. I remember how nervous I was and how my fingernails had disappeared by the end of the game. The best moment was when Roberto Baggio sent his penalty kick flying over the goal. My whole town woke up that midnight. Everyone was out, drums beating, all joyous for a team that was from another continent, but supported by fans as far away as Mombasa, Kenya. I will never forget that night.

Ahmad, Kenya

FAMOUS FOOTBALLING NO-SHOWS

∙∙∙

❝ *One thing is for sure, a World Cup without me is nothing to watch.* **❞**
ZLATAN IBRAHIMOVIĆ

When you turn up or tune in to watch a game of football, you expect there to be two teams in attendance. It's a given. But on a handful of occasions, matches have been missing a vital ingredient – a full set of players. Sometimes for a good reason. Sometimes not.

ESTONIA V SCOTLAND, 1996 WORLD CUP QUALIFIER

Every fan will admit that there have been plenty of games for which their team didn't turn up. By which they mean that while there were people in football shirts on the pitch, they couldn't be sure if they were footballers. But for Scottish supporters in 1996, there really was a team missing from their World Cup qualifier in Tallinn.

The game was scheduled to take place on the evening of 9 October 1996, but the Scots took one look at the floodlighting for the ground and filed a protest. UEFA agreed that the floodlights weren't up to the job and moved the kick-off back to 1 p.m. The Estonians immediately got the hump, claiming that logistical reasons made the switch impossible, although lost television revenues no doubt had something to do with the foot-stamping as well. The hosts refused to change their plans.

So on the morning of the game, the Scots prepared for a lunch-time kick-off and the Estonians for a tea-time one. And at 1 p.m., Scotland duly lined on the pitch. The Tartan Army belted out, 'There's only one team in Tallinn,' striker Billy Dodds knocked the ball forward to start the game, the referee blew the whistle and off the players walked. The fans made the most of the occasion, playing an impromptu game on the pitch, before heading home. Some hours later, showing commendable stubbornness, the Estonian squad turned up for the game.

Scotland expected to be handed a 3–0 walkover, as had happened in the past, but alas, FIFA showed its customary disregard for transparency and predilection for murky decision-making, and ruled that the game be replayed at a neutral venue. The match ended 0–0, meaning that Scotland had kicked off against nobody and still hadn't won.

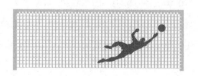

> ### FOOTIE FACT
>
> ....
>
> When La Liga side Sevilla took to the field on Saturday 17 September 2016 to play Eibar, they became the first Spanish top-flight team to start a game without any Spanish players in their line-up. The XI that began the game comprised four Argentinians, three Frenchmen and one man apiece from Italy, Portugal, Brazil and Japan.

USSR V CHILE, 1973 WORLD CUP QUALIFICATION PLAY-OFF SECOND LEG

There was more than a place at the 1974 World Cup in West Germany at stake in Santiago in November 1973. The second leg of this qualification play-off wasn't just a game of football, it was also a battle of political ideologies. In Chile on 11 September 1973, the democratically elected left-wing government of Salvador Allende had been overthrown by a military coup led by army chief Augusto Pinochet.

The first leg of the play-off in Moscow had taken place despite the violent upheaval, and had ended goalless. However, by the time the second leg approached in November, the communist authorities in the USSR were ready to take a stand.

The match was due to take place in the national stadium in Santiago, but in the aftermath of the coup, it had been turned into a brutal detention camp, where opponents of Pinochet were tortured and killed. The Soviets point-blank refused to play the game there. The new regime denied the accusation, so FIFA went to Santiago to inspect the stadium. To its great shame, the representatives of the world football governing body somehow found no evidence of the Soviet claims. As a result, the game would go ahead.

So, on 21 November 1973, the Chilean national team lined up in a sparsely filled stadium against nobody. Good to their word, the Soviets had boycotted the game. Chile kicked off and dribbled down field, with the players somewhat sheepishly passing the ball around, before shooting into an empty net. The celebrations were muted. The scoreboard blazed 1–0 to Chile and the game was over. Chile were going to the World Cup.

MIDDLESBROUGH V BLACKBURN ROVERS, ENGLISH PREMIER LEAGUE 1997

Everyone has pulled a sickie from work at some point in their lives. It's pretty easy to do and you don't get in trouble. The rules are different for football clubs though. Middlesbrough found this out to their cost in 1997.

It's interesting to speculate what was happening at Middlesbrough football club in the December week leading up to their league game against Blackburn Rovers. The team were in the midst of horrendous run of form; they hadn't won a game in over two months and had most recently been handed a drubbing by Liverpool. So the game against fellow relegation candidates Blackburn was of huge significance. But form wasn't Middlesbrough's only problem – according to the club, its squad had been decimated by injury, illness and suspension, with 23 senior players unavailable.

Clearly Middlesbrough were in a bad way and could only have looked upon the game against Blackburn with trepidation. But still, that's what youth teams are for: grin and bear it and give the young players a chance. Manager Bryan Robson didn't agree and just 24 hours before the Saturday kick-off, he announced that his team weren't going to play. He threw a sickie.

You have to wonder who was advising the ex-England captain because it was the mother of wrong decisions. Understandably, Blackburn took umbrage at not being able to play a weakened Middlesbrough side, but the real ire came forth from the Premier League. The following month, it fined the club £50,000 and, critically, docked it three points. Come the end of the season, Middlesbrough were relegated. The gap to safety? Two points.

95

Chelsea hold the record for the highest points total in Premier League history. The London club amassed 95 points when winning the 2004–2005 title. They finished 12 points clear of reigning champions Arsenal and conceded only 15 goals during the entire campaign. The Blues' goalie Petr Čech kept set a record of ten consecutive clean sheets, remaining unbeaten in 24 games overall.

JOHAN CRUYFF AND THE 1978 WORLD CUP

It's not just teams that don't turn up. Johan Cruyff is universally considered one of the world's greatest players and his sublime skills lit up the 1974 World Cup in West Germany, where he had unveiled his famous turn to a global audience. So when Holland qualified for the next tournament, everyone expected the Dutch master to be there.

But he refused to go. His team reached the final again and, agonisingly, lost again. Some blamed his absence for the defeat. So why didn't Cruyff, who was in his prime, turn up? Speculation swirled around the reason for his decision. Was it because of a falling out with the Dutch footballing authorities over sponsorship? Was it his opposition to the right-wing military junta that had seized control of Argentina in 1976? At the time, no proper explanation was forthcoming.

Finally, 30 years after Holland had played the World Cup in Argentina without their best player, Cruyff broke his silence. He had chosen not to go because of a kidnap attempt on his family. He was playing his club football in Barcelona at the time and one evening a few months before the tournament a gang had broken into his flat and tied him and his family up and threatened them at gunpoint.

It should be remembered that kidnapping for ransom or for political purposes was a regular occurrence at the time, with militant groups across Europe snatching prominent figures. Many hostages didn't survive. Sports stars were rarely targeted but the death of 11 Israeli athletes at the 1972 Olympic Games was still relatively fresh in the memory.

Commendably, Cruyff managed to escape and the plot was thwarted. The player and his family were given round-the-clock protection but the traumatic episode clearly had an impact. He said that it had realigned his priorities, and an international tournament on the other side of the world wasn't one of them.

FOOTBALL MOMENT

I will never forget Thursday May 5, 2005. It was the day my club AZ Alkmaar should have reached the final of the Europa League on an epic evening. In the semi-final against big favourites Sporting Portugal, who had won the first leg 2-1 in Lisbon, AZ did what seemed to be impossible in the return game. Cult hero Stein Huysegems scored in the 79th minute in the old Alkmaarderhout stadium to make it 2-1, and another unlikely hero, defender Kew Jaliens, added another goal in extra time; the frenzy reached fever pitch in the stands. I was watching the game in a small bar in Sarajevo, where I was for work, and the locals, who couldn't care less at the start of the game, started supporting the right team when they saw the miracle unfolding! AZ would play a European Cup final, against all odds! But then there was referee Claus Bo Larsen, who decided to add two more minutes to the 120 played. And the dream ended when Miguel Garcia scored in the 122nd minute to make it 3-2, securing a spot in the final for Sporting Portugal on the away-goal rule.

Jan, the Netherlands

Why couldn't you beat a richer club? I've never seen a bag of money score a goal.
JOHAN CRUYFF

BELLES OF THE BALL

·····································

> *The person that said winning isn't everything,*
> *never won anything.*
> **RECORD-BREAKING US SOCCER PLAYER, MIA HAMM**

A BRIEF HISTORY OF WOMEN'S FOOTBALL

Women's football has been around for as long as men's and, like men's, the origins of the women's game are hard to pinpoint. Relics from ancient Greek, Roman and Chinese times portray girls having a kickabout, records from seventeenth century Scotland detail ladies' football matches in 1628 and 1656, and Aboriginal and American cultural artefacts from the 1800s show that it wasn't just men hoofing a ball around.

The turn of the nineteenth century saw women's football become increasingly organised (again mirroring the men's game), with Europe, and Britain in particular, playing a prominent role. One of the early pioneers of women's football was the British Ladies' Football Club, which was founded in 1895 by activist Nettie Honeyball, the pseudonym used by team captain Mary

Hutson. The changes to society brought about by the First World War helped the women's game to flourish further, with British side Dick Kerr's Ladies among the trailblazers of the time, playing games across England and on the continent.

However, having fought furiously in the name of freedom between 1914 and 1919, the British and then the French took away women's right to play the beautiful game. The English FA, whose leadership can safely be assumed to be male and old, handed out a ban in 1921 on the grounds that 'the game of football is quite unsuitable for females and ought not to be encouraged'. The French football authorities followed suit sometime later. Dark days.

It took football associations in Europe the best part of half a century to realise the error of their ways, but once they did, the women's game began to flower again. The ban was lifted in the UK in the late 1960s and women's football associations and leagues were founded across Europe from that time onwards. The seeds were being sown for a footballing revolution.

There have been bumps in the road, not least because financial backing has been, like many a striker, hit and miss, but women's football today is amassing more and more supporters. There are semi-professional and professional women's leagues around the world and a women's World Cup backed by FIFA, a European Championship under the UEFA banner and an Olympic tournament. Interestingly, as the men's game is being choked by obscene amounts of money, a rabid and unhinged media and the greed and ineptitude of administrators, the women's game is offering up football that is in some ways more relatable, and millions of fans are turning up and tuning in to watch it.

150

England's most capped women's footballer is Fara Williams. The Arsenal Ladies central midfielder has played a cap-cupboard-filling 150 times for her country and looks set to add to this impressive tally in 2017. The Londoner made her debut aged just 17 against Portugal in 2001 and has represented England at the 2007, 2011 and 2015 World Cups and the 2005, 2009 and 2013 European Championships.

FOOTIE FACT

English footballing legend Kelly Smith was forced to turn down an invitation to represent England at the 1995 World Cup in Sweden because the tournament clashed with her GCSE exams.

A TIMELINE OF MODERN WOMEN'S FOOTBALL

1895 The British Ladies' Football Club is formed; Dumfries aristocrat Lady Florence Dixie is its patron

1895 The first official women's football match in Britain. North beat South 7–1

1918 The Division 1 Féminine is created in France; the league lasts for 12 seasons before women's football is outlawed

1920   The first women's international match; Preston-based Dick Kerr's Ladies beat a French XI 2–0

1921   The English FA bans women from playing at Football League grounds

1969   The Women's Football Association is formed in the UK, with 44 member clubs

1971   The English FA lifts its ban on women playing on Football League grounds

1971   The first Women's Football Association Cup final is held in the UK; Southampton beat Stewarton Thistle 4–1

1972   The first official women's international in the UK is played; England beat Scotland 3–2, and Sylvia Gore goes down in history as the first goalscorer

1974   The women's La Liga in Italy is established; the first single national league title is won by Falchi Astro Montecatini

1975   The Division 1 Féminine in France is reinstated

1984   The first UEFA Women's European Championship final is contested by Sweden and England. England loses on penalties

1988   The Primera División de la Liga de Fútbol Femenino in Spain is founded; Peña Barcilona are the first champions

1989   The Japan Women's Football League, known as the Nadeshiko League, is established; the first team to be crowned champions is Shimizu FC Ladies

1990   The Frauen-Bundesliga is formed in Germany; the first league champions are TSV Siegen

1991   The Women's Football Association launches a national league in the UK, starting with 24 clubs

1991   The FA in England launches the Women's Premier League Cup

1991   China hosts the first women's World Cup; the USA are the inaugural world champions

1992   The FA Women's Premier League is launched in the UK

1996   Women's football makes its debut at the Olympic Games in Atlanta; the USA wins the first gold medal

1997   The Chinese Women's Super League is founded; the first champions are Guangdong Haiyin

2001   UEFA launches the Women's Cup competition; the first winners are German side Frankfurt, who beat Umeå IK of Sweden

2007   Arsenal becomes the first British side to win Europe's top club prize, the UEFA Women's Cup; in doing so, they claim an unprecedented Quadruple, which also includes the FA Women's Premier League Cup, the FA Women's Cup and the FA Women's Premier League

2009   The UEFA Women's Cup is rechristened the UEFA Women's Champions League; the first winners are German team Turbine Potsdam

2009 The Copa Libertadores de América de Fútbol Femenino, or Women's Libertadores, is founded for women's teams in South America; Brazilian side Santos are the inaugural champions

2011 The FA Women's Super League, an eight-team summer competition, is launched in the UK; Arsenal are the first winners

2012 The National Women's Soccer League is founded in the USA; the first champions of this professional competition are Portland Thorns FC

2015 The Iraqi Women's Premier League is established; the inaugural champions are Ghaz Al-Shamal, from Kirkuk

2015 The final of the FA Women's Cup is played at Wembley Stadium for the first time; Chelsea beat Notts County Ladies thanks to a goal by South Korean midfielder Ji So-yun

2015 The USA claims its third World Cup title in Canada, defeating Japan 5–2 in the final

2016 Germany defeat Sweden to take the women's football gold medal at the Rio Olympics

2017 FIFA plans to launch the FIFA Women's Club World Cup, which will feature the six continental club champions and the host nation's club champions

FOOTIE FACT

The largest victory in a women's World Cup football match is 8–0. It has happened twice: Sweden trounced Japan at the 1991 tournament in China and Norway demolished Nigeria at the 1995 competition held in Sweden.

SCANDALOUS BEHAVIOUR

Records show that on Fasting's eve in 1656, drunkenness and fighting was witnessed during men's and women's football games in Scotland. Proper fitba 'en pal.

In 2004, FIFA President Sepp Blatter proposed skimpier kit to boost the profile of women's football. 'Let the women play in more feminine clothes, like they do in volleyball', were his enlightened words.

USA goalkeeper Hope Solo, the most capped international No. 1 of all time, was banned for six months in 2016 for calling the Swedish team that had knocked the Stars and Stripes out of the 2016 Olympics on penalties 'a bunch of cowards'.

352

Striker Kristine Lilly retired from international football in 2010, having made a record-breaking 352 appearances for the USA. It is highly unlikely that this total will ever be topped. During this time, she scored a whopping 130 goals for Team USA, won two Olympic gold medals and picked up a World Cup winners' medal. She was inducted into the US Soccer Hall of Fame in 2015.

FIVE OF THE GREATEST WOMEN FOOTBALLERS

① MARTA VIEIRA DA SILVA

When someone says Brazilian, small, quick, strong, creative and considered the greatest footballer of all time, most people would think Pelé. But there's another: Marta. Heralded as the best player women's football has ever seen, the girl from Dois Riachos holds the record for the most goals scored at the World Cup and was voted FIFA World Player of the Year every year between 2006 and 2010. Her club career has spanned multiple teams in Brazil, Sweden and the USA, during which time she has collected a staggering amount of trophies. A striker, she has over 100 goals for her country and has scored more than 350 times at club level, including 210 in 103 appearances for Swedish side Umeå IK.

➋ MIA HAMM

An American soccer legend, Hamm amassed an extraordinary 275 caps for the USA. She first took to the field for the Stars and Stripes aged 15 in 1987 and announced her retirement 17 years later after winning gold for her country at the Olympic Games in Athens. When she hung up her boots, she had scored a then-record 158 international goals and had been integral to a period of US dominance of the women's game. Hamm can look back on an international career that includes two World Cup winners' medals (1991 and 1999) and two Olympic titles (1996 and 2004). She also has Olympic silver and two World Cup bronzes, and was named FIFA World Player of the Year in the first two years the award was given, 2001 and 2002.

➌ ABBY WAMBACH

Mia Hamm's world record for international goals stood until her compatriot Wambach passed her in 2013. By the time she retired in 2015, after a 14-year career, the New York-born striker had notched up an unbelievable 184 goals in 255 appearances for her country. Those strikes helped Team USA to win two Olympic golds (2004 and 2012) and one World Cup title (2015). She is also a World Cup runner-up and two-time bronze medallist. In 2012, Wambach added the FIFA World Player of the Year award to an already heaving mantelpiece, becoming the first American to get the prize since Hamm ten years previously. Perhaps Wambach's most famous goal is the one she scored to send America's 2011 World Cup quarter-final against Brazil to penalties. The two sides had played 122 minutes of football and the Brazilians were seconds away from victory. But Wambach levelled with a header and the USA triumphed in the shootout.

❹ KELLY SMITH

Just how good was Kelly Smith? She was a pioneer for the women's game in England. Despite an injury-ravaged career, Smith still regularly made the headlines for her football, collecting trophies and accolades as she went. American soccer great Mia Hamm described her as 'different class' and former England manager Hope Powell compared her with Maradona and Messi. Starting out in the game in 1994, she hopped back and forth over the Atlantic as leagues and teams came and went, wowing crowds everywhere she landed. She set records in the US in the late 90s and was an integral part of the Arsenal Ladies team that dominated British and European football in the mid-2000s. In her glorious second spell with the London club, Smith scored an incredible 73 goals in 66 appearances. She brought her England days to an end in 2015, bringing to a close a 20-year international career that included 46 goals in 117 caps and appearances at the 2007 and 2011 World Cups. She also represented Great Britain at the 2012 Olympic Games in London.

❺ CHRISTINE SINCLAIR

If Abby Wambach's international goalscoring record is going to be broken it will be by the prolific Canadian striker Christine Sinclair. The 12-time Canadian Player of the Year and six-time FIFA World Player of the Year nominee has helped to put Canadian women's soccer on the map. Making her international debut at just 16 years old, she has represented her country at multiple Olympic tournaments and World Cups. Her goals were key in securing a hugely impressive fourth place finish for Canada at the 2003 World Cup and a bronze medal at the 2012 Olympic Games. Her performance in London also earned her the tournament's Golden Boot award for top goalscorer. Sinclair's club career has been focused in North America, where she has won championships with three different teams: FC Gold Pride, Western New York Flash and Portland Thorns FC.

0.72

Former USA striker Abby Wambach holds the world record for scoring goals on the international stage. She scored 184 goals at a rate of 0.72 per game. The men's leading goalscorer, Iran's Ali Daei (109 goals in 149 games), has a ratio of 0.73. Landon Donovan, who is the USA men's side's most prolific forward, has ratio of 0.36.

THE CELEBRITY FOOTBALLER

> *" In 1969, I gave up women and alcohol –*
> *it was the worst 20 minutes of my life. "*
>
> **GEORGE BEST**

Today, the game's top players are automatically thought of as celebrities – there is little if no transition between the two worlds. Sponsorship deals, glossy ads, Sunday newspaper exposés, weddings in *Hello!* magazine – it's the norm not the exception. But there was a time when things were different.

MR BEST, WHERE DID IT ALL GO WRONG?

The celebrity footballer isn't a new concept. Indeed, it's one that goes back further than many may think, before Becks, before Best. Sir Stanley Matthews, who made his senior debut in 1932, is often referred to as one of the greatest English players and he can also lay claim to being the first celebrity footballer.

Matthews enjoyed a glittering career at club and national level, but in the era of the maximum wage (no more than £20 a week), his earning power from the game was limited. So, he looked to use his stardom to boost his income: he popped up in short films, such as one for the Co-operative Wholesale Society promoting the boots that he endorsed, and print adverts, including one for Craven 'A' cigarettes, even though he was a famous non-smoker. He also wasn't a stranger to the front pages. After he retired, he tried his hand at management, including, at the time of apartheid, an all-black team in Soweto. Around the same time, he also very publicly left his wife for a local interpreter he met on a sponsor's tour to Czechoslovakia. He went on to marry the woman, who was later accused of being a Soviet spy.

Of course, on the infamy scale, it's hard to beat George Best. For all his footballing ability, he is known as much for his appetite for glitz, glamour and women. It all did for him in the end, but he left a canon of anecdotes, quips and quotes. If Matthews entered new territory by lending his name to a few products, then Best all but invaded this new land of opportunity. There were fashion shops, potato snacks, exercise LPs (with a Miss World, naturally), comics and much, much more. Plus there was the legendary lifestyle, which is summed up rather nicely by an off-the-cuff comment from a bellboy. The bellboy, on delivering champagne to the footballer's hotel room, only to find him in his bed with a scantily clad Miss World, covered in the winnings from a big night at a casino, muttered the words: 'Mr Best, where did it all go wrong?'

BEERS NAMED AFTER FOOTBALLERS

- On Le Tiss – brewed by Brewhouse & Kitchen, which is only a decent toe punt from St. Mary's Stadium, this golden ale is a tribute to legendary Southampton striker Matt Le Tissier.

- Radabeer – this beer from Leeds Brewery was named after former Leeds and South African captain Lucas Radebe. 10p from every pint went towards transfer funds for the stricken Yorkshire club.

- Gazza's Tears – this mighty Somerset cider (12%!) is a tribute to infamous Geordie and England footballing genius Paul Gascoigne and turns up regularly at the Newcastle Beer Festival.

- Vardy's Volley – brewed by craft beer boffins Steamin' Billy, this light ale celebrates the goalscoring exploits of England striker Jamie Vardy that propelled Leicester to the English Premier League title.

GOLDENBALLS, THE MAN WITH THE MIDAS TOUCH

If Matthews was a pioneer and Best a hedonistic explorer, what does that make David Beckham? The all-conquering force? The odd sarong and sex scandal aside, a footballer's celebrity wattage has never shone so bright and so purely. It says something that the clouds that have dimmed this light have been caused by his actions on the field rather than off it. His is a whole different type of footballing celebrity.

There was a time, back in the 1990s, when he was just a young footballer making waves at an up-and-coming Fergie-led Manchester United. But that didn't last long. Before we knew it, he was the centre of the universe. Scoring outlandish goals for fun, marrying one of the world's biggest pop stars, getting married on a purple throne, wearing sarongs, showing off a new haircut every five minutes, carrying the England team on his shoulders, etc. Everything he did was news.

And little has changed. Today he is an industry, a universe of his own. Having overcome the odds in Spain, he brought football back to the States and starred in glittering cameos in Paris and Rome, before hanging up his boots, bringing down the curtain on a 20-year career that included 19 major trophies.

Not that his star has waned in retirement. No running a boozer for him. Indeed, his fame has only grown brighter. Among the things keeping him busy are the David Beckham UNICEF Fund and the Miami Major League Soccer club, of which he is co-owner. He also popped up as a projectionist in the 2015 film *The Man from U.N.C.L.E.* How long before he becomes a 'sir'? Those odds have to be pretty short. Or president of the world? Don't bet against it. This is the level that Becks has taken his football celebrity to. He has gone further than any footballer before him: he is now a pure, 24-carat gold celebrity.

57

Scoring from your own half used to be the rarest of footballing feats. Pelé had tried and failed at the 1970 World Cup, but the mere attempt was a sign of his genius. No one had seen it done. Manchester United's David Beckham changed everything in 1996. Seeing the Wimbledon keeper off his line, the boy wonder launched a rocket, the halfway line approaching, and scored. How far away was he? An incredible 57 yards.

TALES OF THE UNEXPECTED (AND EXPECTED)

In an era of such titles as the 'Official Robot Partner of Manchester City', the 'Official Diesel Engine Partner of Manchester United' and the 'Official Coffee, Tea and Bakery Provider of Liverpool', it comes as no surprise to see players' faces in often silly adverts. While famous footballers advertising airlines in Russia, office equipment in South Korea or mobile phones in Malaysia may look ridiculous, everything is polished, the rough edges all squared away. Perhaps we can blame Gary Lineker and the crisps for that. But there was once a time when a footballer's presence in an advert was both far less common and far less predictable.

Remember George Best? He liked 'birds and booze' as much as football. He wasn't shy of lending his name to a product or two, although many didn't quite match his lifestyle choices.

Take his advert for Cookstown sausages – 'Only one thing gets George Best away from football… Cookstown family sausages' went the jingle (really, George?). He also championed the merits of milk (if only it had been a case of the white stuff and not the hard stuff).

Talking of which, Gazza didn't mind using his football fame to feather the nest a bit. His Brut aftershave advert is a peach: fresh from his World Cup 1990 theatrics, a splash or two is enough to get him turning a burly bunch of noisy road workers into a mini-urban orchestra. Kevin Keegan, who was one of England's best players before he became one of its poorer managers, also has form when it comes to getting in front of the camera in return for some corporate shilling. His advert for Brut deodorant with British heavyweight boxer Henry Cooper is up there with that volleyball scene in *Top Gun* in terms of unintentionally homoerotic celluloid gold. The two work out furiously together and then join each other for a jolly old time in the shower, telling us how great Brut is.

It's easy to laugh, but at least advertising deodorant or the local pub (yes, really, with Bobby Moore) probably had some credibility with teammates. I'm not sure that can be said for Chicken Tonight (England and Arsenal's Ian Wright, pretending to be posh); Unipart oil filters (the great Pat Jennings of Arsenal and Tottenham, dressed as one while playing in goal); Danepak bacon (Manchester United's Great Dane Peter Schmeichel, singing and playing a range of instruments); or Just for Men hair dye (Portugal legend Luís Figo, faffing with his hair a lot). The money must have been good.

But adverts have proved that footballers aren't all a mercenary bunch, sort of. Kevin Keegan popped up in a 1970s public information film about the Green Cross Code, giving out some sage advice to children, while wearing a pair of incredible flares. Legendary football pundit Jimmy Hill did one around the same time for a motorcycle safety campaign, and a chillingly professional piece of work it was too. Is there a modern equivalent? Well, a while back Pelé did an advert for an erectile dysfunction drug. Does that count?

FOOTIE FACT

Footballing adage: How do you make a small fortune in football? Start with a big one.

THE MARVELLOUS MAN FROM MADEIRA

Cristiano Ronaldo is adored the world over, by football fans, by brand managers, by a lot of people. Hugs from the Portuguese have been known to cause recipients to lose the power of speech; a signature from the uber *galáctico* has been known to cost the world's biggest brands millions. And he does this while being a little bit hard to like.

He's not very cuddly. And that's not because of his muscles, which he likes to show off regularly, being all big and poky. It's because he seems to have a World Cup-sized ego. Just check out the museum in his home town of Funchal dedicated solely to the life and times of Portugal's number seven. But to be as good as he is – and he is one of the greatest footballers the game has ever seen – perhaps that's unavoidable, part of the job description. He is without doubt an arch individualist in a team sport. There was always going to be some friction.

And the comparisons with Lionel Messi – a quieter, more modest genius who is very much a team player – don't help assuage the accusations of arrogance. Yet what does Ronaldo care? He is immensely successful and immensely wealthy. He typifies the modern football celebrity and is the model to which all others aspire. His private life is largely just that, private. Anything controversial usually stems from his actions on the pitch rather than off it. This is the image that allows him to earn millions in sponsorship deals. He is the best paid footballer in the world, earning $80 million in 2015 according to Forbes. He has a contract with Nike that pays him $13 million a year alone. Then there are endorsement deals past and present with Armani, KFC, Emirates, TAG Heuer, Coca-Cola, Castrol and Konami.

Back on the field: where to start with Ronaldo's achievements while playing for Manchester United, Real Madrid and Portugal? Well, in club football, he's won multiple league titles, domestic cups, Champions Leagues and FIFA Club World Cup trophies in England and Spain. He has the record for the most goals scored in a single Champions League season (17 in 2013–2014) and in 2015 became the all-time top goalscorer in the competition. Nobody has scored more goals for Real Madrid and the Portuguese captain is the fastest player to score 200 goals in La Liga (it took him just 178 games). His individual awards could fill a museum (and do).

At international level, he is a European Championship-winning captain, having led his country to their international trophy in 2016. In addition, he holds the highest number of appearances at the tournament and is the first player to find the back of the net at four tournaments in succession. Following his victorious summer in France, he also holds the record with Michel Platini for the most goals scored at a finals. Does he enjoy sharing this summit? Probably as much as he likes sharing the limelight with Messi. So, come the next Euros, only a fool would bet against a 35-year-old Cristiano making sure that he sits alone atop of this golden goalscoring tree.

Ronaldo is without doubt one of the finest players to have ever graced a football field. While debate about the world's best player still revolves around Pelé and Maradona, it can't do for too much longer. Once Ronaldo hangs up his boots, the old guard will surely have to make room for the man from Madeira. Maybe if Messi wasn't playing at the same time, he would already be there. It is easy to take Cristiano's feats for granted such is the ease and speed at which he scores goals and breaks records, but when he and his famous sparring partner finally retire, football will be a much poorer place.

But Cristiano won't be on his uppers. It seems unlikely that a dodgy investment or two will down him. His carefully constructed, expertly managed type of footballing celebrity – alien to the eras of Matthews, Best, Gascoigne and to some extent Beckham – has made sure of that.

508

Before he set out to celebrate beating West Germany in the 1966 World Cup final, England defender Jack Charlton slipped a note into the breast pocket of his suit. To make sure that he got back to his own bed, or at least somewhere close, he wrote: 'This body is to be returned to Room 508, Royal Garden Hotel.' It didn't work. He woke up on the floor of a stranger's house in Walthamshow.

MONEY, MONEY, MONEY

> ❝ *When I heard my agent repeat the figure of £55,000 [per week], I nearly swerved off the road. 'He's taking the piss, Jonathan!' I yelled down the phone. I was trembling with anger.* ❞
>
> **ENGLAND DEFENDER ASHLEY COLE, IN HIS AUTOBIOGRAPHY, ON HEARING A WAGE OFFER FROM THEN EMPLOYERS ARSENAL FC**

'They've paid how much!?' is a frequent refrain of the football fan. No season is complete without a few exorbitant transfer fees. But it wasn't always thus. The concept of the football transfer is nearly as old as the game itself, but for a few years before player registration was introduced, when they could turn out for any side, whenever they fancied. If that's unimaginable now, you have to wonder what nineteenth-century fans would make of the sums swapped for players today.

A TIMELINE OF THE FOOTBALL TRANSFER

1893   The first three-figure transfer: Willie Groves moves to Aston Villa for £100

1905   Middlesbrough pay £1,000 for Alf Common

1922   Syd Puddefoot leaves West Ham for Falkirk for £5,000

1928   Arsenal pay Bolton £10,890 for the services of David Jack

1961   Luis Suárez is the first six-figure signing; Inter Milan pay £152,000

1975   Giuseppe Savoldi leaves Bologna for Inter Milan for £1.2 million

1979   Trevor Francis is the first British £1-million man, signing for Nottingham Forest

1982   Barcelona break the world transfer record; Maradona signs for £3 million

1985   Napoli break the world transfer record; Maradona signs for £5 million

1996   Newcastle sign Alan Shearer from Southampton for £15 million

2000   Luís Figo swaps Barcelona for Real Madrid for £37 million

2001   Zinedine Zidane is signed by Real Madrid for £46.6 million

2001 Gianluigi Buffon is the most expensive goalkeeper of all time at £30 million

2002 Rio Ferdinand is the world's most expensive defender at £29.1 million

2009 Brazilian Kaká switches from Milan to Real Madrid for £56 million

2009 Cristiano Ronaldo leaves Manchester United for Real Madrid for £80 million

2011 Chelsea smash the British transfer record: £50 million for Liverpool's Fernando Torres

2013 Gareth Bale moves from Tottenham Hotspur to Real Madrid for £85.3 million

2014 David Luiz takes the crown for the world's most expensive defender at £50 million

2014 Luis Suárez leaves Liverpool for Barcelona at a cost of £75 million

2016 John Stones becomes the costliest British defender, joining Man City for £47 million

2016 Gonzalo Higuaín joins Juventus from Napoli for £75.3 million

2016 Paul Pogba re-signs for Manchester United for £93.2 million

515.3

Manchester United are the first British football club to earn half a billion pounds in a year. The Old Trafford giants posted revenue of £515.3 million for 2015–2016. However, the Red Devils weren't the first to break the half-billion mark – that was Spanish side Barcelona, whose annual earnings for the same period were a Brexit-boosted £570 million.

A TALE OF TWO MILLIONS

It won't be long before football welcomes its first £100-million player, so before this moment comes to dominate talk of football transfer history, it seems a good time to celebrate the footballer whose transfer was the first to break the £1 million mark.

The first thing to do is give the fanfare to the right player, because a common mistake is to attribute this financial bauble to England's Trevor Francis, who swapped the blue of Birmingham City for the red of Brian Clough's all-conquering Nottingham Forest for £1.1 million in 1979. In fact, the honour belongs to a lesser-known Italian striker by the name of Giuseppe Savoldi.

Savoldi beat Francis to the tape by a good four years when Napoli signed him from Bologna for a world-record fee of two billion lire (£1.2 million) in 1975. However, of the two players, Francis wore his crown with more distinction. While Savoldi maintained a strong scoring record at Napoli and then back at Bologna, he failed to net a regular place in the national team, earning just four caps. In contrast, the English striker can look back on, among others, a European Cup winner's medal, a Super Cup winner's medal and a Coppa Italia winner's medal from his time in Italy, as well as 52 caps for England, including a couple of goals at the 1982 World Cup.

Interestingly, both million-pound men had short stints at Italian club Atalanta in the 1980s, both scoring a single goal in a handful of appearances. However, they never played together, missing each other by a couple of years.

FOOTIE FACT

Swedish striker Zlatan Ibrahimović is the world's most expensive player by accumulated transfer fees. The total paid to date for his services by the likes of Juventus, Inter Milan, AC Milan, Barcelona and Paris Saint-Germain? A staggering £150.5 million.

GARETH BALE: THE WELSH MARADONA

It's fair to say that Gareth Bale has managed the €100-million-man tag well. Spanish giants Real Madrid splashed the eye-bulging amount of cash for the next-generation Welsh Wizard in 2013, continuing its tradition of *galácticos* (world-famous players signed for mammoth fees) and breaking the world transfer record that it had previously set in 2009 on signing Cristiano Ronaldo from Manchester United for £80 million.

Since arriving in Madrid, Bale has notched up two UEFA Champions League winners' medals, becoming the first Welshman to score in a final, bagged a sensational winning goal in the 2014 Copa del Rey final against Barcelona and claimed the 2014 UEFA Super Cup. He has also scored a hatful of goals in La Liga, Spain's equivalent of the Premier League, becoming the highest scoring British player in the competition in the process.

He has also delivered for his national team, driving Wales to a historic semi-final in the 2016 European Championship. Captaining the side, his goals against Slovakia, England and Russia helped Wales to top their group and earn a place in the knockout phase, where they would conquer Northern Ireland and Belgium before falling to eventual winners Portugal. For his efforts, he would earn the nickname 'Garadonna', a reference to the mighty Maradona, who almost single-handedly won Argentina the 1986 World Cup.

So, how did the only Welsh *galáctico* make his way from South Wales to the Santiago Bernabéu? Well, it all began at a Cardiff Civil Service under-nines six-a-side tournament. Bale the boy wonder was spotted by a scout from Southampton, as he glided past opposition players like they weren't there and hammered in or set up goal after goal. This was the moment that would set in motion a journey in which the latest stop is one of the world's greatest football clubs.

His first professional club was the Saints on the south coast, where the winger started out as a left back, at the tender age of 16. Just over a year after becoming the second youngest player to turn out for Southampton, during which time he became known more for his creativity and free-kick taking than his defending, he was signed by Tottenham Hotspur. It was at White Hart Lane that his career truly took off, although it wasn't all plain sailing. His first few seasons were interrupted by injury and it wasn't until the 2011–2012 season that this star began to really shine, helping Spurs progress in the Champions League and picking up the Professional Footballers' Association (PFA) Young Player of the Year award.

From there on in, the eyes of the world's media were firmly fixed on Bale as he began to dominate games in the way only great players do. Goals and awards flowed, before the men from Madrid arrived with an offer he and Spurs couldn't resist.

REAL MADRID'S GALÁCTICOS

Real Madrid is famous for its *galácticos*. The club may have eased up a little on its outlay of late, but the talent that has put on the famous white shirt has been truly incredible. Here is a pick of the best and most influential of recent times.

2000 Luís Figo arrives from Barcelona for £37 million

2001 Zinedine Zidane signs from Juventus for £46.6 million

2002 Ronaldo moves from Inter Milan for £30 million

2003 David Beckham leaves Manchester United for £25 million

2005 Sergio Ramos departs Sevilla for £18 million

2007 Gonzalo Higuaín arrives from River Plate for €12 million

2009	Kaká joins from AC Milan for £56 million
2009	Cristiano Ronaldo is prised away from Manchester United for £80 million
2009	Karim Benzema signs from Lyon for £30.8 million
2009	Xabi Alonso leaves Liverpool for £31.2 million
2010	Ángel Di María arrives from Benfica for £21 million
2012	Luka Modrić moves from Tottenham Hotspur for £33 million
2013	Gareth Bale joins Los Blancos for then world record £85.3 million
2013	Isco leaves La Liga rivals Málaga for £23 million
2014	James Rodríguez signs from Monaco for £63 million
2014	Toni Kroos switches Bayern Munich for the Bernabéu for €30 million
2015	Mateo Kovačić leaves Inter Milan for €32 million

FOOTIE FACT

There was a time when a footballer's wage was so small that players had to have a job outside the game. The story goes that 1940s and 1950s England legend Sir Tom Finney would turn up to a home game with his plumbing tools in a wheelbarrow, and once he was done terrorising the opposition's defence, he'd pick them up again and head off to finish the job. Not something you'd find Lionel Messi doing today.

6.8

Manchester City bought John Stones from Everton for £47.5 million in August 2016, making him the world's second most expensive defender. The transfer triggered a sell-on fee for the England player's first club, Barnsley, which received £6.8 million as a result of the Blues' ambition. The sum received by the Yorkshire club was almost £2 million more than it made in the whole of the previous year.

GAMES THAT ROCKED THE WORLD

> *He can't kick with his left foot, he can't head a ball,*
> *he can't tackle and he doesn't score many goals.*
> *Apart from that, he's all right.*
> **GEORGE BEST ON DAVID BECKHAM**

Football is full of drama – big upsets, big victories, big bust ups – but there are games that stand out even from these moments. These are the where-were-you-when matches, the ones whose results touched the lives of those outside the frenzied fiefdom of fandom. These are 90 minutes that have rocked the world.

BRAZIL V GERMANY, 2014 WORLD CUP SEMI-FINAL

Germany didn't beat a Brazil team that embodied the beautiful game on 8 July 2014 (which was what Paolo Rossi's Italy had done in 1982) – but still, this Teutonic victory at the World

Cup was a hammer blow that sent shockwaves through the footballing world.

Brazil were the hosts and had scraped their way to a last-four match against a strong German side. Luiz Felipe Scolari's men were expecting a tough game and they got one. As wake-up calls go, it was a 100-decibel primal scream. Looking back the signs were there. Brazil were under pressure from the start to perform in their own backyard, painfully aware of the misery suffered by the nation at the last World Cup in Brazil in 1950, when they had lost in the final in front of 200,000 people. Nevertheless, the team had advanced, thanks to a mixture of old-fashioned luck, generous refereeing and the stand-out skill of a couple of players. And for the big game against Germany those stars were missing: leading scorer Neymar, injured from the quarter-final against Colombia, where a tackle had broken a bone in his back, and the team's defensive lynchpin Thiago Silva, suspended after picking up his second yellow card of the tournament in the same game. Their absence would be telling. Very telling.

The semi-final was all over after 30 minutes. Germany blew away their opponents, reshaping the footballing universe as they coolly slotted home goal after goal. The Germans were as ruthless and efficient as the Brazilians were disorganised and delirious. In an astonishing six minutes, the Brazilian keeper picked the ball out of his net four times. And one of the Germans to put the ball there was Miroslav Klose, who in doing so scored his 16th World Cup goal, breaking the record held by Brazilian hero Ronaldo. Every strike was a heartless, brutal puncturing of Brazil's footballing ego.

The Brazilians were utterly shambolic. As the first half drew to an end and the scoreboard lasered 5–0 brightly into the Rio night, it was hard to tell which set of players was more astonished. The Germans reportedly agreed to take it a bit easier in the second half but they still dominated and scored two more goals. Brazil's consolation in the last minute really wasn't anything of the sort.

There were tears long before the final whistle, by which time most Brazilian fans were past denial and anger and well into depression and acceptance. Brazil had lost 7–1 in a World Cup semi-final on home soil and it had been a horror show – one of the most embarrassing defeats in the competition's history. Germany had torn their opponents to shreds. Brazilian football and the way the world perceived it would never be the same again.

ENGLAND V HUNGARY, 1953 INTERNATIONAL FRIENDLY

In retrospect, English football fans should be grateful for the masterclass that Hungary gave to their team on a damp afternoon in November in 1953. The result, and more so the nature of it, lead to a rebuilding of English football that would result in World Cup triumph in 1966. However, as the final whistle blew to mark the end of a game that redefined England's position in world football, the emotion that engulfed Wembley Stadium and the country was not gratitude but staggering disbelief.

International football was still in its infancy in the early 1950s and despite a chaotic showing at the 1950 World Cup, England still regarded themselves as one of the sport's superpowers. This lofty self-regard was based largely on the belief that the country that had invented the game had to have the best systems, tactics, coaches and players. A sterling record in England – the Three Lions had not lost to a team from outside the UK at Wembley – was testament to this superiority. As far as the FA was concerned, England was the home of football with international competitions to be treated with an attitude bordering on contempt (the first World Cups were given short shrift and the team's star player was late for the 1950 competition because he was on an FA goodwill tour of Canada).

This pomposity was well and truly pricked by Hungary and the insularity and complacency of the English game brutally exposed for the whole world to see. There had been signs that the English way of playing, fixed rigidly to the 3-2-5 W-M formation (in which the defenders form a 'W' and the forwards an 'M'), was becoming outmoded and was unable to deal with the fluid style being adopted by more and more foreign teams. Yet, true to form, those that ran English football refused to countenance that their methods could be bettered. So it was not just the England team that was swept aside by Hungary that afternoon, but also the certainties that had propped up English football for decades.

Hungary annihilated England, smashing their opponent's proud home record to smithereens. The 6–3 scoreline didn't do the Hungary side justice – the Magyars, led by one of football's all-time greats Ferenc Puskás, should have scored more as they totally outclassed their rivals. England were run ragged, unable to cope with an innovative style of play that featured positions such as false nines and deep-lying midfielders. The final whistle felt like an act of mercy by the referee.

As the dust settled, it was clear that the defeat was not a freak occurrence that could be brushed aside and forgotten with a shrug of acceptance in the knowledge that the status quo would soon be restored. The result shook English and world football to its core (any lingering suspicion that the loss had been an accident was banished the following year as Hungary dished out a 7–1 thumping to England in Budapest). Yet every cloud has a silver lining, and the upside of the crushing defeat in 1953 for England was that their right back on that afternoon would one day become manager of the national team. His name: Alf Ramsey.

DENMARK V GERMANY 1992, EUROPEAN CHAMPIONSHIP FINAL

Walking off the pitch after a 2–1 victory against Northern Ireland in November 1991, Danish players no doubt gave thought to the following summer. They had won their final European Championship qualifying match and the tournament was taking place in Sweden. Yet not one would have dreamt of holding the trophy aloft in Gothenburg, having cast aside the reigning world champions Germany. They wouldn't have done so for the simple reason that they had failed to qualify.

Despite the late-autumn win, Denmark had finished behind Yugoslavia in their qualifying group and with only the group winners progressing to the finals, the only football the Danish players could look forward to the next summer was any they might play on the beach. Furthermore, the qualifying campaign had seen a raft of star players either quit or banished, and had ended with the manager seemingly bound for the door marked *Do one*. Danish football was not in a good way.

However, football is a funny old game. In the months leading up to the tournament, with the situation deteriorating in Yugoslavia, there was a growing feeling among the Danish players that they might need their boots that summer after all. And they were right. A matter of days before the start of the competition, UEFA expelled the Yugoslav team and asked Denmark to replace them.

It was a dramatic decision, not least because of the timing. Yugoslavia were a strong team that were more than capable of making a mark on the tournament. In contrast, while Denmark were an acceptable substitute, with little time to prepare, they weren't expected to do anything memorable. The general consensus was that a decent showing in the group stage, where they were pitted against two strongly fancied sides in England and France, and hosts Sweden, would be an achievement in itself. And after a draw against England and a loss to Sweden, this prediction looked about right. Yet, what happened next had the world rubbing its eyes in disbelief.

The Danes weren't expected to trouble the French, who could count on the industry and imagination of Deschamps, Papin and Cantona, so the win the Scandinavian side needed to qualify for the next round seemed highly unlikely. Yet with a pre-game round of mini-golf under their belts, the Danish side were 1–0 up within five minutes and walked off the pitch 2–1 winners and European Championship semi-finalists. As a reward, the coach treated his players to a fast-food feast.

Their last-four game would be against reigning tournament champions Holland, which boasted some of the world's best players in Rijkaard, Gullit, Bergkamp and van Basten. Surely this would be where the Danish dream would end? Two Larsen goals and a flawless display of penalty-taking meant otherwise. A tournament decider with Germany was booked.

If Denmark were expecting a storm in the final, they got one, with a dominant Germany throwing everything at them. But the big Danish keeper stood tall, almost single-handedly keeping the Germans at bay. A man-of-the-match performance from the No. 1 Peter Schmeichel and one goal apiece from Jan Jensen and Kim Vilfort made the fairy tale come true. A team that weren't meant to be at the competition was going home with the trophy.

FOOTIE FACT

The Southampton side that played in the English First Division in 1982 contained six past and future England captains. They were Mick Channon, Dave Watson, Peter Shilton, Kevin Keegan, Mick Mills and Alan Ball. Despite this pedigree, which included a World Cup winner and a European Cup champion, the south coast club could only finish 12th.

PORTUGAL V GREECE 2004, EUROPEAN CHAMPIONSHIP FINAL

The underdogs had had their day in the European Championship in 1992, but there could never be another Denmark moment, could there? Greece turned up to the 2004 competition as rank outsiders. It was an unfair tag as they had qualified strongly, pipping Spain to top spot, but still, Greece were a team made up of domestic and European journeymen – they weren't going to win. Bookmakers certainly didn't think so, giving odds of 80–1 and upwards against such a feat.

The group in which the Greeks were drawn suggested their trip to Portugal would be a very short one. Not only were they pitted against the powerful if ageing hosts, but also familiar foes Spain and a never-to-be-underestimated Russia. Their first game was the tournament opener against the Portuguese, and Greece were expected to play the role of proud loser, gallantly put to the sword by Luís Figo's local heroes, who included a new boy by the name of Cristiano Ronaldo. But the Greek side, managed by German Otto Rehhagel, was having none of it. They comprehensively crashed the party and came away with a well-deserved 2–1 win.

The footballing apple cart was well and truly upset. Next came a battling draw against Spain, but after little more than 15 minutes of their last group game against Russia, it seemed that the hope ignited by the victory against Portugal would be extinguished. A Russian side with nothing to play for were two up against an unusually attack-minded Greece. Over in the other game, the Iberian giants were playing out a scoreless draw. Rehhagel's men were heading home. So who saved Greece? Step forward Portuguese substitute striker Nuno Gomes. His goal gave Portugal the win against Spain and meant Greece qualified for the quarter-final by the slenderest of margins: the Greeks and the Spaniards had finished on the same points with the same goal difference, but Greece had scored two more goals.

A well-organised, workmanlike team had already surpassed expectations but with reigning European champions France up next, few people outside of Greece expected Rehhagel's men to extend their stay. They wouldn't be a match for a Gallic side that boasted European footballing aristocracy such as Zidane, Henry, Thuram and Makélélé. But they were. The score was 1–0 to Greece and not for the last time. In fact, that was the result in the semi-final against the Czech Republic. The Czechs had lit up the tournament playing some of the most eye-catching football it had ever seen, so a victory against the less than aesthetic Greeks seemed a formality. There was no way lightening was going to strike twice. Well, it did. 1–0 to Greece.

Greece were one game away from doing the unthinkable but there was one last chance for sanity to be restored and for football to make sense again. The final would see the Greeks play hosts Portugal again, a repeat of the opening game. If ever there was a scenario that shrieked redemption it was here. This was the last throw of the dice for Portugal's so-called golden generation and while they had lost unexpectedly against Greece at the beginning of the tournament, here was the opportunity to right that wrong and give the country a fairy tale to recount for the ages. Except the fairy tale would belong to Greece. The score? 1–0 of course. The world looked on agog. The rank outsiders were champions of Europe.

11

The World Cup quarter-final between Argentina and England in 1986 witnessed perhaps the competition's greatest goal. And it involved no hands, just a blur of legs. Diego Maradona spins away from two England midfielders in his own half and heads for goal. Outpacing everyone, he slaloms past two defenders and slots it coolly past the keeper. How long did it all take? Eleven glorious seconds.

❝ *The goal was scored a little bit by the hand of God. Another bit by the head of Maradona.* ❞

DIEGO MARADONA

TEN OF THE WORLD CUP'S GREATEST UPSETS

❶ ENGLAND V USA, 1950

Is this the daddy of all World Cup shocks? Quite possibly. England are high on their own supply, telling anyone who'd listen that theirs is the best football in the world. They've brushed aside Chile in their opening game and now face the USA, a rag-tag team of part-timers. Such is the confidence that Stanley Matthews is allowed to continue on a promotional tour of Canada. Fans at home await an avalanche of goals but the first newspaper reports say 0–1 to USA. *Nah, that can't be right*, thinks just about everybody. It must be a misprint. Surely it's 10-1 to England. But no, it really was Pomposity 0 Football 1.

❷ NORTH KOREA V ITALY, 1966

Today North Korean detonations shake the world for the wrong reasons but in July 1966, the Chollima were responsible for one of the World Cup's great explosions. Italy were not at their strongest after a harrowing start to post-war international football, but they were still expected to swat aside World Cup debutants that had no footballing pedigree. For most of the first half there was little reason to think that an upset was coming: Italy were out of sorts but still dominant. But just before the whistle, Pak Doo-ik scored to put the cat among the pigeons. The second half carried on in a similar vein but North Korea held on for an historic victory.

❸ SPAIN V NORTHERN IRELAND, 1982

This was the first tournament to involve 24 national sides and as a result, there were smaller teams in attendance, including Northern Ireland. The Irish started solidly and a win in their last group game would send them through. Just one problem: it was against hosts Spain, who would go on to contest the final of Euro 84. In a strongly partisan Santiago Bernabéu, Billy Bingham's side were given little hope, but that's all they needed. Gerry Armstrong scored just after half-time and the boys in white and green hung on, with ten men for the last 30 minutes, for a stadium-silencing win.

④ ALGERIA V WEST GERMANY, 1982

Before Northern Ireland sent Spain packing, Algeria threatened to do the same to West Germany. The Germans were the reigning European champions and were expected to make light work of the African minnows in their opening game. Instead they got the mother of all wake-up calls. The lumbering Germans just couldn't deal with the lightning speed of Algeria's counter-attacking. When Rummenigge equalised an opener from Madjer, everyone waited for Germany to run riot, but the Desert Warriors flew up the pitch straight from the restart and grabbed the lead back. And that's the way it stayed. The Disgrace of Gijón would do for Algeria in the end but they'll always have this game.

⑤ ARGENTINA V CAMEROON, 1990

Cameroon were footballing small fry and Argentina were reigning world champions, captained by none other than Maradona. So there could only be one result, right? Wrong. A dull game is remembered chiefly for the Africans' attempts at tackling: Argentinian striker Caniggia was memorably sent rocketing into orbit by a particularly wild lunge that earned its exponent a red card. However, by the time this sending off left Cameroon down to nine men, the match was all but over.

Against all the odds, the Indomitable Lions had got themselves in front – a soft header squirming past a red-faced Pumpido in goal – and they kept themselves there. Roar.

❻ COSTA RICA V SCOTLAND, 1990

Scotland were once international tournament regulars (yes, really) and this World Cup pitted them against Brazil and Sweden in a tough group that also included Costa Rica. Yet the Scottish were still confident, especially as they were playing the Central Americans first. What could go wrong? Well, for a side long associated with World Cup ignominy, the obvious did. To be fair to Scotland, competition debutants Costa Rica didn't deserve the no-hopers tag – they'd come through a very tough qualification stage – but still, Scotland should have done better. Alas for the Tartan Army, they could only watch as Los Ticos soaked up the pressure and scored on the break.

❼ SENEGAL V FRANCE, 2002

In the grand French tradition of either majesty or malcontent at international tournaments, 2002 was a case of the latter. However, as reigning world and European champions, no one expected it. Surely an opening game against competition new boys Senegal would be a formality, even without an injured Zinedine Zidane. Les Bleus had a real shot at retaining the trophy. Yet they didn't get close. Papa Bouba Diop's goal for the Lions was a scrambled one but it still cast a dagger into the heart of French ambition. The world stood shocked and France fell apart. They finished bottom of the group and bid the World Cup an early *adieu*.

8 ITALY V SOUTH KOREA, 2002

South Korea were joint hosts in 2002 but were expected to do little. So when they got to the knockout stages, the general feeling was 'well done, but you're not beating Italy'. What followed was one of the most controversial games in World Cup history. The referee did not have a good day at the office – among the raft of questionable decisions, the red card for Totti in extra time is all kinds of ludicrous. Yet it should never have mattered. Italy should have been out of sight by the time Seol Ki-hyeon levelled with two minutes to go. A 117th minute Ahn Jung-hwan winner would stun the world and send the home nation wild.

9 SPAIN V SOUTH KOREA, 2002

The world had barely enough time to digest South Korea's defeat of Italy before the co-hosts faced Spain in the quarter-finals. Lightening couldn't strike twice? Surely the Red Devils had used up all their luck in the game against the Azzurri? They hadn't. How Spain didn't score is one of the modern world's great mysteries, but two incorrectly ruled out goals didn't help. Conspiracy theorists would have a field day, especially those in southern Europe. The game went to penalties and after a truly dreadful spot kick from Joaquín, Hong Myung-bo ensured that he'd never have to buy a soju again and sent his team to the semis. Cue pandemonium.

⑩ NEW ZEALAND V ITALY, 2010

New Zealand didn't actually beat Italy but it must have felt like a defeat for the Azzurri. The All Whites' World Cup show reel is pretty short and, until this game, lacked much in way of highlights. New Zealand were rank outsiders (2000–1 outsiders in fact) making their first appearance at the tournament for 28 years, while Italy were reigning champions with back-to-back wins on their mind. The favourites were without stars Pirlo and Buffon, but still. The Azzurri would equalise a shock All Whites opener but they couldn't muster a winner. After a frenzied final few minutes, the whistle went and New Zealand fans partied like it was 1966.

ROY'S BOYS DONE BAD (ENGLAND V ICELAND, ROUND OF 16, EURO 2016)

Did this game shake the world? Well, Europe certainly shook, and not just because of the Icelandic thunder clap. England had once again messed up the group stage, coming second when topping it didn't look like too much to ask. But the gods were smiling on the Three Lions, or so they thought, because they were handed a second-round tie against minnows Iceland. Even the deeply disillusioned English were full of confidence.

And they were even more bullish after four minutes of the match, when captain Wayne Rooney tucked away a penalty. Victory beckoned yet only ignominy arrived. The bubble was burst just 180 seconds later and then smashed to smithereens on 18 minutes. 2–1 to Iceland, but there was still over 70 minutes left. Roy's Boys would come back, right? Nope. And it never looked on the cards. The longer the game went on the more bewildered and clueless the much-feted and much-moneyed England players looked. A star-less side drawn from a population of just 300,000 whose manager was a part-time dentist stood firm. The European Championship had one of its biggest ever shocks.

PLAYERS THAT SHOOK THE WORLD

· ·

> ❝ *In music there is Beethoven and the rest.*
> *In football there is Pelé and the rest.* ❞
> **PELÉ**

Every week a player will do something incredible – a gravity-defying save, an audacious trick, an unbelievable goal – and one of the main reasons these acts are so utterly amazing is the fact that they happen in isolation. The player involved doesn't make a habit of it. However, there are a very small number of players for whom performing something special is standard operating procedure.

JOHAN CRUYFF – THE TOTAL FOOTBALLER

Getting people to agree on the world's best player is usually an exercise in futility. The debate between Pelé and Maradona will rage on forever (or at least until Messi and Cristiano Ronaldo retire). However, when it comes to handing out the bronze medal in this hotly contested competition, there is rarely any argument at all. It's easy, it's Johan Cruyff.

Ranking Pelé and Maradona automatically above Cruyff is done perhaps largely because the Brazilian and the Argentinian both drove their countries to World Cup glory, whereas the Dutch master could only manage to get Holland into second place. Yet Cruyff arguably had a greater impact on the game. He revolutionised it as a player and as a manager.

The Dutch striker's defining moment as a player came in the 23rd minute of the 1974 World Cup group match between Holland and Sweden. Cruyff has the ball high up on the left side of the pitch, just outside the penalty area, and facing towards his own goal, is being tightly marked. All of a sudden, he uses the instep of his right foot to sweep the ball back inside his standing left leg, before spinning 180 degrees and tearing away. The Swedish defender is left trying to tackle thin air, lost in time and space to a piece of trickery that almost seemed to defy the laws of physics. The world of football looked on agog as the Cruyff Turn was born. The game would never be the same again.

Cruyff took the perceived wisdoms of the game and so thoroughly debunked them as to make them seem like archaic beliefs belonging to an ancient world. He showed the world a new style of playing that combined technical mastery and creative genius to deliver a game that was both more aesthetically pleasing and more lethally unanswerable. His was a style based on possession, high-tempo short passing and a fluidity that meant players could occupy any outfield role. Cruyff had introduced the world to Total Football. And as a player, it served him well, earning him a historic three European Cup wins in a row with Ajax as well as eight Dutch league titles and five Dutch Cup victories. He also won La Liga, the Spanish league, and the Copa del Rey, Spain's League Cup, with Barcelona.

By the time he moved into management, he had already thrust the game well and truly into the future, but he was far from done. Keen to take his playing philosophy from the pitch to the dugout, Cruyff began implementing his ideas as coach of Ajax. But it was in the next job in Catalonia that his school of football really took shape. His achievements as manager of Barcelona are relatively modest by current club standards – although winning four La Liga titles in a row is an extraordinary feat in any era – but it is Cruyff's foundations that today's empire is built on.

The way of playing he introduced, the possession-based football, or tiki-taka, has brought Barcelona and Spain enormous riches. Not only did he introduce a style of play, but perhaps even more importantly, he established the fabled academy at La Masia that has produced the likes of Lionel Messi, Xavi Hernández and Andrés Iniesta. Football is a religion in Spain and the rivalries are fittingly fervent but every Spanish fan has reason to worship at the church of Cruyff. He didn't just make the Oranje boom or Barça beyond brilliant, he changed football forever.

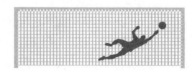

FOOTIE FACT

Marco Materazzi holds a unique World Cup quadruple. In the 2006 final against France, the Italian defender gave away the penalty that gave France a 1–0 lead, scored the equaliser for the Azzurri ten minutes later, was instrumental in the sending off of Zinedine Zidane and successfully slotted home a spot kick in the shootout that decided the game in favour of Italy. Busy.

Messi is an alien that dedicates himself to playing with humans.

JUVENTUS CAPTAIN GIANLUIGI BUFFON AHEAD OF THE CHAMPIONS LEAGUE FINAL IN 2015

LIONEL MESSI – LEO, KING OF THE JUNGLE

What is there to say about Lionel Messi? Well, for one he must get on Cristiano Ronaldo's wick. For every superhuman feat the Portuguese achieves, the supremely gifted Argentinian is there to do something even more super. The Real hitman's CR7 museum would have to be a lot bigger if it wasn't for his Barcelona rival. Also, everyone seems to like him more.

Messi is the team player, both playmaker and goalscorer, to the Ronaldo soloist. Yet despite this, they have plenty in common, not least vying for the title of the greatest footballer on the planet. The Argentinian continues to keep his nose in front in this race but the title is still very much up for grabs, especially with the Madrid man helping his country to European glory in the summer of 2016. Messi has represented Argentina in three Copa América finals and a World Cup final, captaining the side on three of these four occasions, but has lost them all. Fine margins.

Still, at club level, Lionel is untouchable. And it almost didn't happen for the boy from Rosario. As a youth team player in Argentina, he was struck down by a hormone deficiency that affected his growth and with domestic clubs unwilling to foot the medical bill to help him, his career was in serious jeopardy. That's when Spanish giants Barcelona stepped in and agreed to pay for this treatment. Never has there been a better investment in football. Messi has helped establish the Catalan club as the world's supreme side, collecting major trophies and awards at a frankly obscene rate.

He has won everything there is to win with Barcelona, including in 2008–2009 all six trophies that the team competed for. He is a serial La Liga, Champions League, Copa del Rey, UEFA Super Cup and FIFA Club World Cup winner and the only player to have scored in six different club competitions twice. He is also the only player to have scored more than 40 goals in seven consecutive seasons and has won more FIFA Ballon d'Or awards than any other player in history. Furthermore, he is the record goalscorer in El Clásico clashes (Barcelona v Real Madrid). The roll of honour goes on and on and on.

So, what is there left for Messi to achieve? Well, for starters, international glory with Argentina, which you suspect will come, and there's also keeping Cristiano in the shade, which is a battle that is likely to have plenty more twists and turns. And the title of the greatest footballer of all time? Sorry, Ron, but you fancy it's his to lose.

THE FACTORY WORKER FROM FUENTEALBILLA – ANDRÉS INIESTA

The unassuming Spain midfielder is no ordinary factory worker. A product of the revered La Masia (the Factory) training academy at Barcelona, Iniesta is considered one of the best players ever to have graced a pitch.

The footballer from Fuentealbilla has come to epitomise the tiki-taka football that has fired Spain and Barcelona to such giddy heights. He is the embodiment of the possession, quick passing-based football instilled at Barcelona by Johan Cruyff and resurrected by Pep Guardiola. Both his club and national side have enjoyed such dominance thanks to his innate genius and the majesty with which he has orchestrated play in the red of Spain and the famous stripes of Barcelona.

Where's the proof? Just look at what the Iniesta production line has churned out. For his club, there have been eight La Liga titles, four Champions League trophies and three FIFA Club World triumphs between 2004 and 2016. This period has included two historic trebles, in 2009 and 2015. You can also chuck in four Copa del Rey gongs and three UEFA Super Cup wins. And he's still plying his trade for Barcelona, so expect his medal haul to grow.

For his country, the roll call of achievements is just as incredible, if not more so. Iniesta was integral to Spain winning its first piece of major football silverware in 2008. Alongside teammate Xavi, he pulled the strings that enabled La Furia Roja to bring home the European Championship for the first time. Four years later, he and Spain went one better. In a bravura display, Spanish tiki-taka overcame Dutch brutality to claim the World Cup on a historic night in Johannesburg. At the heart of this victory was Spain's rainmaker and it was his goal in extra time that eventually separated the two teams.

If there was any doubt as to Iniesta's skills and Spain's superiority, they were quashed in 2012 when the reigning European and world champions retained the European Championship title. Again, the architect of every step, including a drubbing of Italy in the final, was Iniesta. A midfield mastermind quietly, efficiently and effectively going about the business of being one of the greatest players in the world.

> *I find it terrible when talents are rejected based on computer stats. Based on the criteria at Ajax now, I would have been rejected. When I was 15, I couldn't kick a ball 15 metres with my left and maybe 20 with my right. My qualities, technique and vision, are not detectable by a computer.*
>
> **DUTCH FOOTBALL MASTER JOHAN CRUYFF**

91

Lionel Messi holds the record for the most goals scored in a calendar year. In 2012, the Barcelona playmaker found the back of the net an extraordinary 91 times, beating the 1972 record held by German goal machine Gerd Müller. Messi's goals-per-game ratio was an incredible 1.319. He also has the record for goals in a single season (82). Prolific.

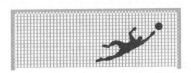

THE JOY OF FOOTBALL GROUNDS

• •

> ❝ *Wembley is the cathedral of football. It is the capital of football and it is the heart of football.* ❞
>
> **PELÉ**

When it comes to the joy of football, part of it is to be found in the stadiums where the game is actually played. Going to watch your team play and stepping inside the stadium is to become part of something bigger: there's a reverence to it, a bristling sense of anticipation, an electricity to the events that connects you in a completely different way to watching on television.

And then there's playing in a stadium. As a kid kicking a ball around a park, with makeshift goalposts and the pitch as wide as the patch of grass you're playing on, and even as an adult toiling away on potato fields or boggy hillsides at the weekends for an amateur side, you dream of playing at a proper football ground, with its terraces, floodlights and groundkeepers.

Not that every stadium is the same, far from it. The charm is in what makes visiting each one a unique experience, even in this age of the identikit ground.

3,637

Despite their status as minnows of Latin American football, the Bolivian national team has a very strong home record. A main reason for this domestic fortitude is the fact that their stadium, the Estadio Hernando Siles in the capital La Paz, is located at an altitude of 3,637 metres above sea level. Altitude sickness normally kicks in at around 2,500 metres.

THE WEMBLEY WAY

The greatest stadium in English football is undoubtedly Wembley. It is a ground that is steeped in history and inspires awe not just nationally but across the world. Part of the mystique that surrounds and defines Wembley is that to play there is an achievement in itself. To see your team walk out on to the famous pitch means that they are taking part in a showpiece game, whether a semi-final or a final; they've fought hard to get there. A game here holds with it the chance of glory.

Wembley is also the home of the England football team and there are few football-obsessed English kids that won't have imagined themselves lining up before the game, belting out the national anthem and going on to score the winning goal. To play for your country is what every young player thinks about when they pull the shirt, shorts and socks on for the first time. And if you're English, this dream is irrevocably linked to Wembley.

Of course, there are two Wembley stadiums these days. The original, completed just days before it hosted its first FA Cup final and initially known as the Empire Stadium, was built for a country whose belief in its status in the world was unshakeable. Football was no different and Wembley with its famous Twin Towers was a monument to England's lofty position in the game.

Of course, to borrow a phrase from Sir Alex Ferguson, English football was knocked off its perch, but Wembley remained hallowed turf up until the decision was made to rebuild it from scratch. If the new Wembley doesn't have the same soul, it is no less imposing. The second largest stadium in Europe, with its roof and arch visible across London, it is very much a modern wonder.

WEMBLEY MILESTONES

1923   The original Wembley Stadium hosts its first FA Cup final between Bolton Wanderers and West Ham

1924   The first international game is played at Wembley. England draw 1–1 with Scotland

1948   The stadium plays host to the 1948 Olympic Games

1951   The first England international match at Wembley not involving Scotland takes place. Argentina are beaten 2–1

1963   Wembley welcomes the European Cup final for the first time as AC Milan overcome Benfica 2–1

1966 · Wembley is the venue for the World Cup final as England defeat West Germany in extra time to lift the greatest prize in football

1968 Wembley hosts its second European Cup final, with Manchester United becoming the first English winners

1996 England hosts Euro 96 and the final at Wembley sees Germany win 2–1 against the Czech Republic, with a golden goal in extra time

2000 The last FA Cup final at the old Wembley takes place: Chelsea beat Aston Villa 1–0

2000 The old Wembley sees its last England international, with the Three Lions losing 1–0 to old foes Germany

2007 The first competitive game is held at the new Wembley: Stevenage Borough beat Kidderminster Harriers in the non-league FA Trophy

2007 The first England international takes place at the new Wembley: England draw 1–1 with Brazil

2011 The new Wembley hosts its first Champions League final: Barcelona defeat Manchester United 3–1

2013 Borussia Dortmund and Bayern Munich contest the second Champions League final at the new Wembley, celebrating 150 years of the FA

2020 Wembley will host the final and semi-finals of Euro 2020, the first time the competition will be played on a pan-continental basis

FOOTBALL GROUNDS: THE UNUSUAL AND THE UNBELIEVABLE

Every supporter has their own theatre of dreams. From the Camp Nou in Spain where thousands regularly come to worship Barcelona to the Maracanã in Brazil that embodies the style and history of *jogo bonito*. Whether they're old grounds whose rough edges and rudimentary structures are testament to another era or sparkling new stadiums that are symbols of a hopeful future, they are all cathedrals of football. And they are all different. Although some are more different than others.

Every stadium has its quirks, whether major or minor.

- Until a couple of years ago, when you visited AFC Bournemouth, you'd find a ground with only three sides – the fourth was open, with the trees that lined that end offering those willing to climb the chance of watching for free.

- Go to Brisbane Road, home of Leyton Orient, and at each corner you'll see a block of flats, whose terraces almost protrude into play.

- Head to the ground of Luton Town to support your team and to get into the away end you have to enter through some terraced houses.

Of course, it isn't just British grounds that are unusual. It's a worldwide phenomenon.

- Perhaps one of the most striking football grounds in the world is the home of Portuguese team Braga. The stadium was built in a quarry, seemingly squeezed in between giant slabs of rock. There is seating on only two sides, with one end a craggy cliff face and the other offering views of the city below. Its relative newness – it was constructed for the 2004 European Championship – only adds to the sense of marvellous oddity.

- From one rock formation to another: the Omnilife stadium in Guadalajara, Mexico, soars out of the earth like an erupting volcano, with its white roof the ring of smoke hanging above the crater. The local landscape was the inspiration behind this incredible stadium.

- The Janguito Malucelli stadium in Brazil takes the link with nature even further. It is the country's first eco-friendly football ground: there is no hard metal seating, just seats embedded in the grassy hillside, and reclaimed wood is used throughout with no concrete in sight.

- If you played football in your back garden as a kid, chances are that you had to pay regular visits to your neighbours' gardens, officially or surreptitiously, to retrieve your ball. Scrambling over a fence or two was part of the fun. So imagine playing at the Vesturi á Eiðinum in Vágur in the Faroe Islands. As close to the rugged coastline as you can get without toppling into the water, the stadium employs people in boats to fetch wayward shots.

■ From by the water to on it: that's where the multi-purpose Marina Bay Float Stadium in Singapore can be found. As its name suggests, this football pitch has actually been built on the water, which in this case is the Marina Reservoir. The world's largest floating stage, with fan seating for up to 30,000 positioned just back from the waterside, the platform is made entirely of steel and can take the weight of up to 9,000 people. Which is plenty for a game of football.

31

Coffs Harbour International Stadium saw history made in April 2001. The 2002 World Cup qualifying match played that day in New South Wales witnessed an incredible 31 goals. Australia scored all of them. The team on the wrong side of this almighty hammering – a record victory in international football – was American Samoa. In obliterating their opponents, the Socceroos had beaten their own record, a 22–0 win over Tonga, which they had set 48 hours earlier.

FOOTIE FACT

The highest ever attendance at a football stadium? Some reports say that over 200,000 people were in the crowd for the first FA Cup final at Wembley in 1923. A similar number is thought to have crammed into the Centenario stadium in Uruguay to watch the 1950 World Cup final between Uruguay and Brazil.

MANAGERS: THE BEST AND THE WORST

> *Rome wasn't built in a day but I wasn't on that particular job.*
>
> **BRIAN CLOUGH**

Football's heroes and villains aren't just found on the pitch. They're in the dugouts too. Worshipped or vilified, there is no shortage of theatre: a manager is either the master puppeteer who guides their team to glory or the inept meddler who is the cause of their side's failure. Over the length of a career, a manager can regularly switch identities. The eccentric, the egotistical, the enigmatic, those at the end of their tethers: there's never a dull moment.

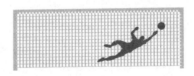

7

Only seven people have won the European Cup/Champions League as both a player and a manager. The very special seven are Zinedine Zidane, Josep Guardiola, Frank Rijkaard, Carlo Ancelotti, Johan Cruyff, Giovanni Trapattoni and Miguel Muñoz. Together this gifted group have claimed European club football's top prize an amazing 24 times.

THE BEST BOSSES IN THE BUSINESS

How do you choose the game's best managers? How do you judge success? By the amount of silverware in the trophy room? By keeping an unfancied side playing in the top league? By reinventing the way a team plays and creating a whole new footballing philosophy? And then there's your own club bias. Fortunately some managers are just so good that none of this matters.

PEP: THE MASTER OF TIKI-TAKA

The world of football management has seen some iconic figures, but at present few wield a greater aura than Spain's Pep Guardiola. He is the legendary Barcelona midfielder who became the club's even more legendary manager, before taking up the hot seat at Bayern Munich, where he enhanced Die Roten's reputation as a European übermannschaft. Post-Bayern, he has driven his tiki-taka truck to Manchester, putting his name on the manager's door at City's Etihad Stadium.

Guardiola transformed Barcelona and made tiki-taka (a style based on short passes, movement and maintaining possession) into a football phenomenon. In his first season alone, he won the unprecedented Spanish Treble of the La Liga, the Copa del Rey and the Champions League. Over the course of four seasons, he collected a staggering 14 trophies, including an amazing six pieces of silverware within the 2009 calendar year, adding the Spanish Supercopa, the UEFA Super Cup and the FIFA Club World Cup to an already historic haul. He nearly repeated the trick in 2011, only missing out on the Copa del Rey.

In Germany he quickly proved his doubters wrong and successfully blended German steel with his Iberian tiki-taka. In three years in Bavaria, the Catalan won three Bundesliga league titles on the bounce (losing just nine games) and a UEFA Super Cup and FIFA Club World Cup.

His reign at Manchester City has only just begun but it is already clear that the Blues are an even more formidable force than they were pre-Pep. City fans should expect trophies, lots of them.

JÜRGEN THE GERMAN

How can you be a manager of a team other than Bayern Munich in the German Bundesliga and be considered one of the best in the world? By being Jürgen Klopp, that's how. His reign at Borussia Dortmund, and the success that it brought, is emblematic of how a change in philosophy has transformed German football over the past decade.

He turned up at Borussia Dortmund with the club languishing in mid-table and instantly got results: the side won the German

Supercup in his first season. Thereafter he showed that other teams could be as good as perennial champions Bayern Munich. He showed that they could be even better. Dortmund won the Bundesliga championship for the first time in a decade under Klopp in 2011; then they claimed it again in 2012, all the time playing with a style based on youth, attack and confidence.

Now Jürgen the German is Jürgen the Scouser and as manager of Liverpool he is once again charged with reviving an under-performing side and defeating some of the game's giants, including Manchester City, whose manager is old foe Pep Guardiola. With a couple of cup finals already under his belt, he is well on his way to putting the Reds back on their perch.

THE SPECIAL ONE

Or perhaps it should be the 'Busy One' considering the amount of rebuilding that has to be done at Old Trafford. Whatever the nickname, his managerial career, which has spanned Porto, Chelsea, Inter Milan, Real Madrid, Chelsea again and Manchester United, is without a doubt very special. Love him or hate him, he is one of the best managers in the business.

So, where do you start with Mourinho? With the fact that he earned his managerial spurs under the late Sir Bobby Robson at Barcelona? That he guided Portuguese side Porto to Champions League glory? That he turned Chelsea into a dominant force in the English Premier League and Europe? That he won six trophies, including the Italian Treble in 2009–2010, in his three years at Inter Milan? That he won La Liga, Copa del Rey and Supercopa titles with Real Madrid in Spain despite playing against Guardiola's Barcelona? That he restored Chelsea as champions of England in his first season back at the club?

Or with his UEFA Manager of the Year award in 2003 and 2004? Or his FIFA World Coach of the Year award in 2010? Or his nine-year, 150-match, four-club unbeaten home-league record?

And then there are the accolades he has picked up outside the game: *New Statesman* Man of the Year and Spanish *Rolling Stone* Rockstar of the Year, as well as his own children's cartoon in Portugal called *Mourinho and the Special Ones*. Wherever he goes, he wins and that's why the Old Trafford club came calling in 2016.

THE GOVERNOR FROM THE GOVAN

Manchester United's dip in form since Sir Alex Ferguson retired only illustrates just how great a manager the Governor from Govan was. He helmed the club for almost 30 years, a length of time that is simply incredible, and achieved a level of success that puts him in the company of British managerial greats, such as Matt Busby, Bill Shankly and Bob Paisley.

Much is made of the time Ferguson was allowed at Manchester United to nurture a winning team and the fact that any modern manager wouldn't be permitted such grace. However, the Scot had already made his managerial mark and had achieved one of his greatest triumphs. Before he turned up at Old Trafford, Ferguson was manager of Scottish team Aberdeen, where he managed to wrestle the domestic league title away from the clutches of the mighty Celtic–Rangers axis, but, more importantly, he steered his side to European glory.

In 1982–1983, Ferguson led Aberdeen, a relatively small Scottish club, to a European Cup Winners' Cup final, beating the likes of Bayern Munich and Tottenham Hotspur along the way. Spanish giants Real Madrid were the opposition in the showpiece game and few outside Aberdeen expected them to win. But they did, 2–1, becoming only the third Scottish team to claim a European trophy. They went on to defeat European Cup champions Hamburg in the UEFA Super Cup too.

Ferguson's ability didn't go unnoticed and he went on to manage the Scottish national team at the 1986 World Cup before job offers in the top league in England started to pour in. Reportedly turning down the likes of Glasgow Rangers, Arsenal, Spurs and Wolverhampton Wanderers, he eventually said yes to Manchester United. The rest, as they say, is history.

Twenty-six years later, on hanging up his famous hairdryer, he could look back on an Old Trafford dynasty that not only included many great teams, but featured players such as David Beckham, Paul Scholes, Roy Keane, Eric Cantona, Ryan Giggs, Cristiano Ronaldo and Wayne Rooney, and that won 13 Premier League titles, five FA Cups, four League Cups, two Champions Leagues, one UEFA Super Cup and one FIFA Club World Cup.

FOOTIE FACT

No English manager has ever led a team to the English Premier League title. Howard Wilkinson was the last Englishman to steer a club to top-flight victory, with Leeds United in 1992, the year before the Premier League was launched.

WELCOME TO THE CLUB AND GOODBYE

For all the great, lengthy managerial reigns in football, there are also those that were painfully short. Whether through incompetence, impatience or ill fortune, the English game boasts many examples of managers for whom getting their feet under the table proved a distant, unachievable dream.

75 DAYS   René Meulensteen (Fulham, 2013–2014)

67 DAYS   Sam Allardyce (England, 2016)

67 DAYS   Michael Appleton (Blackburn Rovers, 2013)

65 DAYS   Michael Appleton (Blackpool, 2012–2013)

57 DAYS   Henning Berg (Blackburn Rovers, 2012)

55 DAYS   Steve Bruce (Wigan, 2001)

51 DAYS   Alan Shearer (Newcastle United, 2009)

44 DAYS   Brian Clough (Leeds, 1974)

41 DAYS   Les Reed (Charlton, 2006)

40 DAYS   Alex McLeish (Nottingham Forest, 2012–2013)

39 DAYS   Paul Gascoigne (Kettering Town, 2005)

33 DAYS   Steve Coppell (Manchester City, 1996)

28 DAYS   Tommy Docherty (Queens Park Rangers, 1968)

28 DAYS   Paul Hart (Queens Park Rangers, 2010)

13 DAYS   Micky Adams (Swansea, 1997)

9 DAYS   Martin Ling (Cambridge United, 2009)

7 DAYS   Kevin Cullis (Swansea, 1996)

4 DAYS   Dave Bassett (Crystal Palace, 1984)

3 DAYS   Bill Lambton (Scunthorpe United, 1959)

10 MINUTES Leroy Rosenior (Torquay United, 2007)

FOOTIE FACT

Which English team has had the most managers in one season? Manchester City in 1995–1996 takes some beating. The club appointed three full-time managers and two caretaker managers over the course of the season. They were relegated.

Reporter:
So, Gordon, in what areas do you think Middlesbrough were better than you today?

Gordon Strachan:
Mainly that big green one out there.

THE FAMOUS AND THE FOOTBALLING

....

Every fan you ask will say he wants to see lively, open football, but what the fan really wants to see is his team win.
FORMER ARSENAL CHAIRMAN DENIS HILL-WOOD

Seeing a famous fan in the crowd is a strangely illuminating moment. It's like you've been let into a secret. And the sense of wonder is amplified if the relationship is an odd one. Why does Prince William support Aston Villa? How come Cameron Diaz is listed as a fan of Brentford? And what is Mikhail Gorbachev doing following Wigan Athletic? It just makes the beautiful game even more fascinating.

A ROYAL SEAL OF APPROVAL

Why the second in line to the throne is an Aston Villa fan is something of a mystery, but it does mean we can write 'Prince William is a Villain' (it's the club's nickname) without fear of being locked up in the Tower of London. Apparently he has supported the Birmingham-based team since he was young and was given to donning Villa socks for games at Eton (it's not often that Aston Villa and Eton are mentioned in the same sentence). Now, as president of the FA, he has ample opportunity to watch games, although his beloved team are, alas, rarely to be seen in showpiece matches.

The reported choices of his brother and grandmother seem more appropriate: Prince Harry and the Queen are both said to support Arsenal. The geography makes sense – the Gunners are from London – and the club's status as one of football's aristocrats also fits the bill. Maybe William was inspired by his dad: Prince Charles is a confirmed fan of Burnley, which, like Aston Villa, play in claret and blue and whose best days, at the moment at least, lie firmly in the past.

FROM ONE STAGE TO ANOTHER

Actors' choice of football teams can be just as leftfield. Aside from Cameron Diaz's love for the Bees, Tom Hanks is rather unfathomably another famous Aston Villa fan, while how Tom Cruise came to follow Arsenal is something of a head-scratcher. Of course, some affiliations, whether fleeting or diehard, make perfect sense: Hackney-born Ray Winstone is a big West Ham fan, Catherine Zeta-Jones supports Swansea City, the place of her birth, and Sean Bean, heroic in *Game of Thrones* and villainous in *Goldeneye*, and a son of Sheffield, calls Sheffield United his team.

From a 007 baddie to the man, or men, himself: James Bond has several teams, or at least the actors who have played him do. Daniel Craig, the spy's latest incarnation, is a supporter of

Liverpool, a global heavyweight with a grand heritage, much like the character. Timothy Dalton's allegiance is less conventional, much like his spin on the world's favourite spook, with his side being Derby County. Original big-screen Bond Sean Connery is true to his Scottish roots in his support of Glasgow Rangers.

THE POLITICS OF THE GAME

Politicians are football fans too. It can be hard to marry the two worlds, but they have quite a lot in common. For a start, football supporters and MPs enjoy bellowing at the opposition on a regular basis (with its two opposing stands, the House of Commons is almost set up like a football ground) and there is a tribalism about how both act: most invest in a lifelong loyalty to one set of colours and take up views accordingly. Furthermore, football and politics both take the summer off except in extraordinary circumstances.

As with other spheres of famous fandom, politics throws up some interesting allegiances. Former Labour leader Michael Foot was a passionate Plymouth Argyle supporter, so much so that the club made him an honorary player and presented him with a shirt featuring the squad number 90 on his 90th birthday. More recent Labour men, and prime ministers, Tony Blair and Gordon Brown put their support of Newcastle United and Raith Rovers on record. To add some balance, former Conservative No. 10 residents John Major and David Cameron are lifelong Chelsea and Aston Villa fans respectively. The allegiance of the more recent incumbent is presumably owed to the fact that his uncle used to be chairman of the club.

Moving into Europe, it shouldn't come as a surprise that former Italian Prime Minister Silvio Berlusconi is a big AC Milan fan because he owns the club. However, the supposed choice of German Chancellor Angela Merkel is more surprising – she is an honorary member of East German team Energie Cottbus, which currently reside in the fourth tier of German football. French President François Hollande is reportedly a fan of AS Monaco. As for why Mikhail Gorbachev is associated with the Latics, it may have something to do with a visit he is said to have made to the team's ground when he was secretary of Soviet football side Metalist Kharkiv. The fates of Gorbachev and the club remained closely linked: the secretary went on to become the last President of the Soviet Union and as a result Metalist went on to become a Ukrainian team.

SINGING THEIR PRAISES

The world of music is seemingly a more natural partner for football than aristocracy or politics, and there are plenty of musicians who sing their allegiances from the rooftops. Of course, among this chorus of fandom, there is the occasional off-key harmony.

- Michael Jackson – Exeter City
- Robbie Williams – Port Vale
- Fatboy Slim – Brighton & Hove Albion
- Sir Elton John – Watford
- Liam and Noel Gallagher – Manchester City

- Ozzy Osbourne – Aston Villa

- Bob Marley – Tottenham Hotspur

- Suggs – Chelsea

- Bill Wyman – Crystal Palace

- Paul McCartney – Everton

- Ian Brown – Manchester United

- Robert Plant – Wolverhampton Wanderers

- Rod Stewart – Celtic

- Luciano Pavarotti – AS Roma

- Plácido Domingo – Barcelona

- Roger Daltrey – Arsenal

- Sting – Newcastle

- Dr Dre – Liverpool

- Snoop Dogg (aka Snoop Lion) – Barcelona

- Jarvis Cocker – Sheffield Wednesday

- Pete Doherty – Queens Park Rangers

- Slash – Stoke City

FINDING THE RIGHT PITCH

While celebrity football fans are to be found far and wide, a celebrity football player – not a musician or an actor who pulls on the boots for the occasional charity game, but someone who has actually played professionally – is a much rarer beast altogether.

A recent recruit to this very select club is Louis Tomlinson, a member of British boy band One Direction, although his credentials aren't quite bona fide. The Doncaster-born pop star may have turned out for his home town's reserve side, but his appearance has as much to do with raising money for charity and for the financially stricken club as it does with his footballing skills.

Spanish crooner Julio Iglesias, a pinup from a completely differently era, did things the other way round: he swapped belting a ball for belting out a melody. Better known as father of Enrique these days, Iglesias Senior was a mega star in his own right and before he took over the world of pop, he played in goal for the Real Madrid reserve team. Reportedly quite the player, he only hung up his gloves following a car accident.

While Tomlinson and Iglesias can both claim to have played professionally, there are a number of celebrities for whom such status was just out of reach despite their best efforts. Matt Smith may never have become the 11th Doctor in Doctor Who if injury hadn't called time on a playing career that included Leicester City, Northampton Town and Nottingham Forest youth teams, while perennial rocker Rod Stewart and celebrity chef Gordon Ramsay had trials for Celtic and Rangers respectively.

FOOTIE FACT

The Nevilles of Manchester have to be one of the UK's most successful sporting families. Brothers Gary and Phil played for Manchester United and England, winning countless trophies for the former, while sister Tracey, twin of Phil, represented England at netball, appearing at the 1998 and 2002 Commonwealth Games.

GAME CHANGERS

Playing two top sports professionally at the same time is all but impossible these days, such is the commitment that making the grade within just one requires. Go back to the first half of the twentieth century and you'll find plenty of examples of footballers-cum-cricketers-cum-rugby players turning out in multiple sports for local and national sides. Famous examples include William Foulke, a 24-stone, 6-foot 4-inch Shropshire lad who captained Chelsea and appeared for England, as well as playing first-class cricket for Derbyshire; and Denis Compton, an FA Cup and League title winner with Arsenal and an all-rounder with Middlesex County Cricket Club and England.

All of this makes the case of Ian Botham even more incredible. His legendary cricketing exploits require little explanation, but to say he is regarded as England's greatest all-rounder, however, his lesser-known footballing career certainly does. While he was batting and bowling for England and Somerset in the 1980s, he also made a handful of appearances for Yeovil

Town and Scunthorpe United. He scored just one goal in nearly 30 appearances, hitting the back of the net in a game for the Somerset-based Glovers.

12

England stars and Tottenham teammates Glenn Hoddle and Chris Waddle released a single called 'Diamond Lights' in 1987. The song spent eight weeks in the UK Singles Chart, peaking at No. 12. Apparently the title is a reference to floodlights. A follow-up, 'It's Goodbye', would be just that: it only reached No. 92.

FOOTIE FACT

Iceland's record goalscorer Eidur Gudjohnsen is the only player to come on in an international game as a substitute for his father. Making his debut for the national team, he replaced his dad, Arnór, in a friendly match against Estonia in 1996.

ALL THE KIT

....

> **"** *The players couldn't pick each other out.* **"**

SIR ALEX FERGUSON DEFLECTS THE BLAME FOR MANCHESTER UNITED'S SURPRISING DEFEAT AGAINST SOUTHAMPTON IN 1996 BY POINTING THE FINGER AT THE SIDE'S NEW, AND NOW INFAMOUS, GREY KIT. HE ORDERED THE PLAYERS TO CHANGE INTO DIFFERENT SHIRTS AT HALF-TIME. THEY STILL LOST.

Playing football today requires a bag full of kit. Socks, shorts and a shirt are just the start. There's a decision to make about what type of football boots you'll need – long studs, short studs, moulded or AstroTurf boots? – and it'll be wise not to forget your shin pads and some tape to keep them in place. If you're playing in winter, you might want to include some under-armour, gloves and a woolly hat, as well as some Deep Heat. Not to mention a tracksuit to warm up in and, if you're going to be really professional about it, some hand warmers for your pockets. Back when the game as we know it was in its infancy, things were a lot simpler.

KNICKERS NOT SHORTS

When organised football first became a staple of British life in the late nineteenth century, players took to the pitch, not in high-tech kits designed to aid mobility and endurance, adorned with the numbers and names of players and sponsors' logos, but in something more rudimentary altogether. For a start, you didn't wear shorts – it was knickerbockers or long trousers, whose baggy material was often secured with braces or a belt. And there was no deliberating over which pair of fluorescent lightweight boots you were going to put on – footballers in this era played in their everyday shoes or work boots, which were invariably heavy and became even more so in the wet. The height of technology and ingenuity in these days was to nail some leather to your footwear to improve the grip (unsurprisingly it didn't take long for this practice to be outlawed, as flinging your feet around with nails potentially protruding from your boots can't have been the safest).

Talking of safety, it took a while for shin pads to be worn on the football field. Before that you just had to man up and take any blows received, intentional or otherwise. The first shin pads were fashioned out of a cut-down pair of cricket pads and the idea caught on fairly quickly. It would be a while before the shin pad as we know it today was invented and, as football shifted from being the pursuit of the wealthy amateur to the game of the working class around the turn of the twentieth century, financial restrictions led to some novel ways of replicating the bastardised cricket pad, most notably the stuffing of old copies of *Reader's Digest* or any other suitably thick magazine down the front of socks.

Around the same time, as the game became professionalised and more rules were introduced, the concept of boots specifically for football emerged. Made of leather, they were still heavy and rose up above the ankle like modern-day rugby boots. Many also had hard toecaps (presumably, as the balls were equally dense in those days, the extra sturdiness allowed great power and not for any malicious reasons) and you could have any colour as long as it was black.

It wasn't until the 1950s that boots as we know them today, shaped below the ankle, were first introduced. Fast forward nearly 70 years and the trend has come full circle. The latest boots now come up over the ankle. But not all is the same – boots are of every perceivable colour and it's not uncommon to see them personalised with initials, shirt numbers or kids' names. How things have changed.

On the subject of specialised kit, it took over 40 years for goalkeepers to be officially required to wear a shirt that differentiated them from their teammates. That's not to say some effort wasn't made prior to the ruling in 1909: goalkeepers often wore woolly jumpers to set themselves apart from colleagues who did their best to wear tops that indicated they were on the same side. As for gloves, these didn't become a regular piece of kit for goalkeepers until the 1970s, so those hard, heavy balls had to be stopped with bare hands alone.

GETTING SHIRTY

Today, every professional football team has at least three strips – a home, an away and a third kit (should the away kit be too similar to opponents' colours) – and these are changed every couple of years. Every team has its distinctive colour, but has alternatives to avoid clashing with opponents. Back in Victorian

England, kits were a lot less sophisticated; indeed, it took a while for the idea of any type of kit to catch on. Initially players would wear what they could get their hands on and the only indication of what team they played for was a coloured cap or sash.

However, it didn't take too long for standard strips to emerge and the early kits were quite garish as clubs embraced links to schools, universities and other sporting organisations. As the game became democratised and clubs rather than individuals became responsible for supplying kits, this trend changed, with basic colours fast becoming the norm. Around this time, shorts began to be worn rather than knickerbockers or trousers, although they were still referred to as 'knickers'.

Shirt numbering was introduced in the 1930s but, this development aside, football shirts didn't really change much until the 1970s, when clubs pursued individualism with more purpose and started selling replica strips. The decade also saw the advent of shirt sponsorship, although only initially in Europe. German football was an early adopter of shirt sponsorship and in 1973 Eintracht Braunschweig is credited with being the first team to don a sponsor's logo, which somewhat controversially belonged to Jägermeister. The herbal liqueur maker's relationship with the side continued until the late 1980s and included an attempt by the company to get the team renamed Eintracht Jägermeister. However, the German FA wasn't having any of it.

The English FA was far less progressive than most of its continental peers and it rigidly imposed a ban on shirt sponsorship until 1977 when Derby signed a deal with Saab, albeit wearing the logoed tops only once. Liverpool were the first team to wear a shirt featuring a sponsor in a league match – the players' tops had Hitachi emblazoned across them in 1978. Non-league team Kettering Town tried to copy what had been going on for several years in Europe and earn some money from shirt sponsorship in 1976: the side ran out once with Kettering Tyres on their chests, but the FA clamped down on it swiftly with the threat of a fine way beyond the means of such a small club. Kettering backed down, but their place in history was secure.

Today, companies pay millions of pounds for their names to be placed on the right shirts: Barcelona will sport the name of Japanese internet retailer Rakuten on their shirts from 2017 thanks to a deal worth £47.2 million a year (this will replace the contract with Qatar Foundation, which is said to pay £25 million annually). Real Madrid has a shirt sponsorship deal with Emirates Airways worth £32 million per year and Bayern Munich pocket around £30 million every 12 months from Deutsche Telekom. Manchester City (Etihad – £20 million), Liverpool (Standard Chartered – £25 million), Arsenal (Fly Emirates – £30 million), Chelsea (Yokohama Rubber – £40 million) and Manchester United (Chevrolet – £53 million) all have multi-million-pound shirt deals. It's a long way from Kettering Tyres.

FOOTIE FACT

Players' names first appeared on the back of their shirts in the UK in the League Cup final between Arsenal and Sheffield Wednesday in 1993. The practice was adopted in the Premier League from the beginning of the 1993–1994 season.

CAMEROON AND THE RISE AND FALL OF THE FOOTBALL ONESIE

Football shirts, or at least some of them, have long been considered fashion items, whether good or bad. The football pitch or ground is no longer the only preserve of a football shirt and the market for classic replica tops has exploded in recent years. Indeed, there is an example of football getting the jump on the fashion industry. Yes, the onesie was on the football pitch long before it was on the high street. But the innovation from Cameroon (and Puma) didn't last long.

The Cameroon onesie, or skintight leotard depending on how you see it, made its debut in 2004 at the African Nations Cup. Why? Well, perhaps it had something to do with the heat, or maybe it was all in the name of pure innovation? Whatever the reason, FIFA took the utmost umbrage and told the Indomitable Lions to bin the new kits, citing a rule about having separate shorts and shirts. Rather surprisingly (or not as the team had got into hot water over short-lived sleeveless tops in 2002), Cameroon stood their ground and played on in the man-sized Babygros. Not that it did them any good: FIFA docked the side six points from its 2006 World Cup qualifying campaign and hit it with a big fine. Puma rather cheekily coughed up the money and Cameroon relented, as did FIFA eventually, restoring the points on appeal, and that was the end of the football onesie.

FOOTIE FACT

Football has seen its fair share of unusual kit fads, from nasal strips and large dollops of Vaseline on the front of shirts that some think improve air intake, to Alice bands that keep long hair out of the eyes and snoods for cold Wednesday nights in Stoke. Then there's Kinesio Tape from Japan, which supposedly gives players an edge by helping to mend injuries.

8

While the length and width of a football pitch can vary (90–120 metres and 45–90 metres respectively), the dimensions of the goals must always be the same. The rectangular constructions at each end of the pitch must be eight feet high (2.44 metres) and eight yards wide (7.32 metres). Quite big when you think about it.

SPOT ON

······································

> **_We don't consider we lost on football but to a circus turn._**
> **JOCK STEIN, FORMER CELTIC MANAGER**

Has a single aspect of football had such an impact on the game as the penalty? Managers complain about not getting them, referees are fooled into giving them, players miss them, players score them. The way the penalty twists and turns the fortunes of teams, players and managers is incredible. What would the game be like without it? Well, that's a whole other story.

THE STORY OF THE PENALTY

The invention of the penalty kick is credited to a sporting chap from Northern Ireland called William McCrum. Initially ridiculed for his idea, the English football authorities gradually came round to it, with a spate of blatant goal-line handballs that denied certain goals helping to change their opinion.

So, in 1891, the penalty kick was born. Players could take them anywhere along a line that was parallel to and 12 yards from the goal line. The penalty spot didn't make an appearance for another

11 years. Scottish side Airdrieonians are thought to have taken the world's first penalty, while the inaugural Football League penalty was struck by Billy Heath of Wolverhampton Wanderers. He scored as his team walloped Accrington Stanley 5–0.

The next big step in the story of the penalty is the creation of the penalty shootout to decide knockout matches that were level after extra time. Incredibly, the shootout didn't come into being until 1970, almost 90 years after Belfast Bill had come up with the concept of the penalty. Before its introduction, knockout games that finished all square were decided by a replay or a coin toss. Yes, a coin toss.

27

The longest penalty shootout in a major professional competition was contested by Liverpool and Middlesbrough in September 2014. Two goals apiece after 120 minutes, the teams required a record 27 spot kicks to settle this League Cup tie. The Reds of Liverpool were the victors, with Boro's Albert Adomah, taking his second penalty of the shootout, the man to finally miss from 12 yards.

LUCKY TOSSERS

ITALY V USSR, EURO 68 SEMI-FINAL

Only four teams contested Euro 68 but the quartet was a stellar one. World champions England were drawn to play a strong Yugoslavia team, while the other semi-final featured tournament hosts Italy and the Soviet Union, runners-up in 1964 and winners in 1960.

The Italy-Soviet Union game had a healthy dash of subtext. The Soviets had knocked the Italians out of the last World Cup in England and the last European Championship in Spain. The Azzurri were wary of their opponents but itching for revenge. The game was a gritty affair, with defences to the fore as both sides were affected by injuries. There was little that was memorable about the game, with it as uninspiring as the weather, apart from the way it ended, of course.

With the match still goalless after 120 minutes and the penalty shootout still a glint in organisers' eyes, it was a coin toss that would decide who would reach the final. After all the hard work, the blood, sweat and tears, it came down to an arbitrary heads or tails.

The Soviets and the Italians tell the story of the toss differently, but the result was still the same. The captains and a UEFA official or two went to the dressing rooms. The coin was agreed upon apparently after some debate – a peseta, a rouble and a dollar were rejected in favour of a guilder – and either the Italian skipper Facchetti called tails and/or the Soviet leader Shesternyov plucked for heads. It was tails and Italy were through and on their way to becoming champions.

Interestingly, a rumour surfaced not long after that the captains had two goes at the coin toss because the first coin vanished under a grate and that once the flip and game was done and dusted, an official went to search for the missing coin. After a bit of investigation, he found it and what was staring up at him? A head.

LIVERPOOL V COLOGNE, 1965 EUROPEAN CUP QUARTER-FINAL

The 1965 European Cup, the forerunner to today's all-conquering Champions League, was not a stranger to a coin toss, with a number of early ties settled in this fashion. However, by far the highest profile match to go down to heads or tails was the quarter-final between Liverpool and Cologne.

The game between the English and German champions – because it was just the champions that qualified for the cup competition back then – was a mouthwatering prospect. Liverpool had charged to the quarter-finals, dispatching Iceland's finest KR and Anderlecht of Belgium with the minimum of fuss. Cologne had had to fight harder to progress but were still well regarded.

An epic game was expected and an epic game was delivered, just not for the reasons anyone expected. The first leg at the Müngersdorfer Stadion ended goalless, so advantage Liverpool. With a home tie to come, they were the strong favourites to win. But that didn't happen, with the two sides playing out another stalemate at Anfield. So the quarter-final would go to a play-off at a neutral venue in Amsterdam. There were goals this time – four of them. Shared equally between the teams.

After almost 300 minutes of football, Liverpool and Cologne couldn't be separated, so to the coin toss it went. Neither skill nor strategy would decide the identity of the semi-finalist, just sheer, blind luck. Even the coin toss took longer than expected to complete – according to Liverpool captain Ron Yeats, he had called tails but on landing the coin had got stuck in a divot. A re-toss was required, much to the Cologne skipper's displeasure because the coin was falling over on heads. The second flip was successful and so were Liverpool.

FOOTBALL MOMENT

2015 Europa League final, Liverpool v Sevilla. I took my son to watch the match in Basel. When Sturridge's goal went in to take us 1–0 up, some Liverpool fans in the row behind me picked up my son and started throwing him in the air. When everything settled down he was grinning ear to ear, saying, 'Liverpool fans are the best!' We ended up losing the match, but my son became a die-hard Red that day.

Warren, England

IT'S A PENALTY!

The first penalty shootout to take place in England featured Hull City and Manchester United, with the Red Devils victorious. The first player to step up from 12 yards? Another Belfast boy, George Best. In European competition, Honvéd and Aberdeen popped the Cup Winners' Cup's cherry and Everton and Borussia Mönchengladbach did the same for the European Cup. Holland's Honvéd and England's Everton were the winners respectively. All of this happened in 1970.

On the international stage, the first major tournament to be decided by a penalty shootout was the 1976 European Championship. Czechoslovakia downed favourites West Germany in an 11-metre duel that featured perhaps the most famous penalty of all time: the Panenka.

THE PANENKA

The Panenka is common currency these days but on a dizzy June night in Belgrade in 1976, it was the rarest of footballing gems. Czech midfielder Antonín Panenka's audacious penalty was the last kick of the final between unfancied Czechoslovakia and reigning world champions West Germany. When the ball landed, it shook the world.

Panenka had taken a penalty like no one, outside of a handful of people in Czechoslovakia, had seen before. It was almost impudent in its simplicity, yet at the same time unbelievably daring. At the time, goalkeepers dived either left or right in trying to save a penalty. None of them stood still. So, Panenka came up with the idea of chipping the ball into the centre of the goal – with the application of exactly the right speed and weight, the goalkeeper, who would have dived in one direction or the other, wouldn't be close to getting it. Genius. That required plenty of practice, almost two years according to the player himself, mostly against his club teammate and Bohemians Praha No. 1 Zdeněk Hruška.

So, the European Championship final has gone to a penalty shootout and having executed the daring dink only a few times, Panenka steps up to take his team's fifth spot kick. He is facing one of the best goalkeepers of the time, Sepp Maier. Showing the steeliest of nerves, Antonín flicks the ball into the centre of the goal. Maier has committed himself to his left. The ball glides into the net. The goalkeeper looks on in disbelief. Panenka, the Czech team, the world explodes. Czechoslovakia are European champions and a legend is born.

From that moment on, the dinked penalty has been known as the Panenka. Plenty of players have tried to emulate the Czech maestro and while a good number have succeeded – notable homages have been performed by Zinedine Zidane in the 2006 World Cup final and Andrea Pirlo in Italy's Euro 2012 quarter-final – many more have failed, showing that the technique is very far from easy. Antonín's amazing penalty will live forever.

> ❝ *Play for joy and the entertainment of the fans and yourself.* ❞
> ANTONÍN PANENKA'S FOOTBALL MOTTO

ELEVEN TERRIBLE PENALTIES

Scoring from 12 yards with just the goalkeeper to beat – how hard can it be? Well, very hard as it turns out.

① SIMONE ZAZA V GERMANY, EURO 2016 QUARTER-FINAL

There are no shortage of candidates for the worst penalty award in the shootout between Italy and Germany at Euro 2016 – even the normally super-efficient Germans produced some howlers. But the one from Italian striker Zaza, who was brought on in the dying seconds of extra time as a spot kick specialist, is the pick of the dodgy bunch. His run-up suggests he is about to attempt the high-jump, springing up and down on the stop like someone doing a demented running man. He stays on the ground but the ball gets plenty of air, sailing high and wide of the goal. Not such an expert then, Simone.

❷ ROBERTO BAGGIO V BRAZIL, 1994 WORLD CUP FINAL

There is nothing particularly unusual about the Italian playmaker's penalty miss – he blazes high over the crossbar. It's the kind of spot-kick skyrocket that you see every weekend. Yes it was the first time that the final had gone to penalties, but what makes this footballing failure notable is that it cost Italy the World Cup, handing Brazil the trophy for a then-record fourth time. For the famously pony-tailed player, who had almost single-handedly dragged his team to the final, lighting up the competition with his skill and scoring, it was a devastatingly cruel way to finish the tournament.

❸ GARY LINEKER V BRAZIL, 1992 FRIENDLY MATCH

Before Lineker was the presenter of *Match of the Day*, he was an exceptional striker. He banged in goals for England for fun, grabbing a World Cup Golden Boot along the way. With his international career winding down, a penalty in a friendly match against Brazil at Wembley gave him the chance to equal Bobby Charlton's long-standing goalscoring record. His effort was dreadful, a wretchedly scuffed spot kick that asked no questions of the goalkeeper. His 49th England goal would never come.

❹ CHRIS WADDLE V WEST GERMANY, 1990 WORLD CUP SEMI-FINAL

When people look back at England's penalty shootout defeat to West Germany in the semi-final of the 1990 World Cup, it is Stuart Pearce's failure to score that is remembered the most. Which is not really fair. Waddle's miss is a more deserving totem of England's defeat. Pearce was a defender and his shot was at least on target. Waddle's was not. So high over the bar did the shot go from the attacking midfielder, it was in danger of clearing the stadium. That was a much worse penalty.

⑤ THIERRY HENRY/ROBERT PIRÈS V MANCHESTER CITY, PREMIER LEAGUE 2005

When you try something clever in a football game, you better get it right. The line between genius and chump is fine. Henry and Pirès wanted to recreate a Cruyff-Olsen penalty. The Dutch and Danish duo had performed an audacious if simple one-two penalty routine to score: Cruyff knocked the ball forward to his left, Olsen returned it and the Dutch master scored past an astonished keeper. The Arsenal duo failed at the first, with Pirès messing up the pass to Henry to much embarrassment. Definitely in the chump category.

⑥ DAVID BECKHAM V PORTUGAL, EURO 2004 QUARTER-FINAL

This is as much bad luck as poor execution, but still it was a woeful spot kick at a critical time – the two teams trading penalties for a place in the semi-final. Beckham's effort went almost vertically, going so high that the television cameras immediately lost sight of it. The state of the penalty spot certainly didn't help – it was all but detached from the rest of the pitch, like a loose wig clinging on desperately to a bald head. England didn't recover and bowed out on penalties again.

7 JOHN TERRY V MANCHESTER UNITED, 2008 CHAMPIONS LEAGUE FINAL

Your team, of which you are the captain and for whom you've played since you were a boy, are on the brink of their first ever Champions League trophy. All you have to do is score your penalty. What could possibly go wrong? As it turns out, on a rain-swept sodden night in Moscow, a lot. Terry slips as he is taking his penalty, skewering it to the right, where it skims the post and goes wide. Chelsea's glory is snatched away in the cruellest of fashions. The shootout wasn't over but the Blues would miss again and the trophy would be heading to Manchester.

8 ASAMOAH GYAN V URUGUAY, 2010 WORLD CUP QUARTER-FINAL

It was all set up for the Ghanaian striker – Uruguay striker Luis Suárez had saved a shot on the line with his hands, earning himself a red card, and the Black Stars had a penalty to win the game. It was good versus evil, and it was the last kick of the game so there would be no coming back for the South American side. Gyan stepped up to make history, with a goal sending an African team into the World Cup semi-finals for the first time. But his shot bounces off the bar and over, and Suárez celebrates as he heads down the tunnel. The game would go to a penalty shootout and Gyan would score, but Ghana would lose.

⑨ VICTOR IKPEBA V CAMEROON, 2000 AFRICAN CUP OF NATIONS

When is a penalty miss not a penalty miss? When it's this one. The final of the 2000 African Cup of Nations (the African equivalent of the European Championship) between Nigeria and Cameroon had gone to penalties. Nigerian striker Ikpeba steps up to take his team's third spot kick, needing to score to keep their hopes alive, and he slams it against the crossbar, with the ball thudding down against the ground a metre behind the line. But no goal. Why the assistant referee standing a few metres to the left didn't give it is a mystery. Cameroon would go on to celebrate victory while Nigeria would fume at a clear injustice.

⑩ JAAP STAM V ITALY, EURO 2000 SEMI-FINAL

This was an atrocious penalty yet still of the common-or-garden slash-high-and-wide variety. But context is everything. That this game went to a penalty shootout is unbelievable in itself. Holland played against ten men for the best part of an hour and had two penalties in normal time. They missed them both and couldn't score. Surely their impotence from 12 yards couldn't continue? It did and Dutch defender Stam's effort underlined the lengths Holland would go to shoot themselves in their collective feet. Unsurprisingly, Stam's miss wasn't Holland's only one and an astonished Italy would go to the final.

⑪ DIANA ROSS, 1994 WORLD CUP

This one is a gift from the gods. We shouldn't be too hard on Ross: she's a singing legend, not a football one, but still. This was the USA's big football moment – it had never hosted the World Cup before and given its lack of soccer culture, first impressions were everything. Cue the opening ceremony and as part of the glitz and glamour, Ross is to score a penalty. Sure she is singing at the same time, but the keeper isn't going to make any effort to save it and she's a lot closer than 12 yards. This is show business remember. She takes her time, ramping up the theatrics, but then shanks her shot horribly wide. The stadium groans, the world bursts into laughter. Football gold.

AN ALTERNATIVE WORLD

Not everybody is enamoured with the penalty shootout. Almost as soon as the decision was taken to introduce the concept in 1970, someone was working to find an alternative to the test of skill and nerve from 12 yards.

Some suggestions have been better than others. Ideas such as an ever-decreasing number of players during extra time, never-ending extra time and a free kick shootout were thankfully put in the pile labelled *forget it*. It was even put forward that data crunching should be used to decide the game, with most shots on targets, most corners, time in possession, fewest fouls, fewest cards and fewest goalkeeper touches used to calculate the winner. Heaven help us if that one ever lands in an administrator's inbox.

THE GOLDEN GOAL

However, there have been alternatives that have seen the light of day. The most well-known of which is the golden goal. The idea is a simple one and was used at Euro 96 and Euro 2000, and the 1998 and 2002 World Cups. If 90 minutes of football couldn't separate the two teams, extra time would be played as normal (two halves of 15 minutes). However, if one team scored in this period, they would win and the game would be over.

The most famous golden goal was scored in the final of Euro 2000 by French striker David Trezeguet. His 103rd minute strike brought the game against Italy to a dramatic end and meant that France were both world and European champions.

However, like France's time atop the football pile, the use of the golden goal after that night in Rotterdam was short lived. Blamed for encouraging negativity in extra time, the golden goal was binned, to be replaced by the silver goal. This wasn't a great step forward. According to the silver goal rule, if a goal was scored in extra time, play would continue to the end of the half, at which point if an equaliser hadn't been scored, the scorer of the silver goal would be the winners. It made an appearance at Euro 2004, but its career was mercifully short, consigned to footballing history shortly after the tournament.

THE 35-YARD SHOOTOUT

The 35-yard shootout was by far the longest surviving penalty shootout alternative (introduced in the 1970s, it lasted almost 30 years) and it was arguably the most entertaining. However, its existence comes with a sizeable caveat – it was only ever used in North America.

Credit where credit is due to the North American football authorities. For administrators that often get soccer innovation horribly wrong – bigger goals, more balls anyone? – the 35-yard shootout was something of a masterstroke. Again the concept was a straightforward one. If the game was still tied after 120 minutes, the shootout would decide the game. Five players from each team would start 35 yards from the goal and have five seconds to beat the keeper.

This shootout asked more of the players' skills and was a fairer way of deciding games. But the format never left North American shores, meaning that this brainchild remained forever with its parents. Nevertheless, in the days when the likes of Pelé, Beckenbauer and Best graced the North American Soccer League, the 35-yard shootout only added to the otherworldliness of the competition.

FOOTIE FACT

A golden goal also settled the 2003 women's World Cup final. It was scored by substitute Nia Künzer to seal a comeback victory for Germany against Sweden.

EUROPEAN CLUB FOOTBALL

❝ I probably think about death 12 times a day. I measure my life in Champions Leagues. How many do I have left? ❞

ACTOR BILL NIGHY

When it comes to bragging rights, what makes one club team better than another? If we're talking about the top sides, it's who's done best in Europe. Yes, league championships are important and domestic cups look nice in the trophy cabinet, but European success is the ultimate benchmark – and the very best European cup to win (there have been a few over the years) is the UEFA Champions League.

A HISTORY OF EUROPEAN CUP FOOTBALL

1955   The European Champions Cup, or European Cup, is established

1955 João Baptista Martins of Portuguese side Sporting Lisbon scores the first European Cup goal

1956 The first European Cup is won by Real Madrid

1960 The European Cup Winners' Cup is launched, contested by the winners of all European domestic cups

1961 Fiorentina are the first team to win the European Cup Winners' Cup

1967 Celtic become the first British team to win the European Cup

1968 Manchester United are the first English side to claim the European Cup

1971 The UEFA Cup is held for the first time; teams qualify based on their performance in domestic league and cup competitions

1972 Tottenham Hotspur are the victors in the inaugural UEFA Cup final

1985 Juventus become the first club to win all three European cups

1986 Romania's Steaua Bucureşti are the first Eastern European side to win the European Cup

1992 The UEFA Champions League replaces the European Cup

1993 French side Marseille win the first Champions League trophy

1998 The Champions League format is expanded to include the best runners-up

1999   Manchester United are the first British winners of the Champions League

1999   The European Cup Winners' Cup is retired by UEFA; Italian team Lazio are the last winners

1999   The Champions League format is expanded to include up to four teams per country

2005   50 years of the European Cup/Champions League: Liverpool are the winners, claiming their fifth trophy

2009   The UEFA Cup is expanded and rechristened the UEFA Europa League

2010   Spain's Atlético Madrid are the first UEFA Europa League champions

2014   Real Madrid win La Décima – their 10th Champions League trophy

1

Only one football player has scored in seven official club competitions in one season. Step forward Spanish striker Fernando Torres. While plying his trade for Chelsea in 2012–2013, he found the back of the net in the English Premier League, the Champions League, the Europa League, the FIFA Club World Cup, the FA Community Shield, the FA Cup and the League Cup.

THE CHAMPIONS LEAGUE ERA

1992 was full of monumental moments in European football. The Premier League, or Premiership as it was initially known, was launched, and England crashed out of Euro 92 in Sweden without a single point; but perhaps most significant was the decision by UEFA to take its premier European cup competition and go back to the drawing board.

Out went the European Cup. Red Star Belgrade of Yugoslavia was the last side, and only the second from Eastern Europe, to claim the trophy. On a May night in Bari, Italy, a trophy that was soon to be consigned to history was claimed by a team from a country that would suffer the same fate. The replacement was the Champions League, featuring, as its name suggested, a new league format to replace the old purely knockout system. The competition has gone from strength to strength and has become more of a spectacle than its predecessor ever was.

What makes Champions League nights so special? Well, a good place to start is the players. Once upon a time, the only way fans watched footballers from different continents was at the World Cup. OK, a handful of stars from places as exotic as Brazil or Argentina, or even Poland or Russia, made it to top European clubs, but that was about it. The Champions League changed the picture, its growth, both physical and financial, driving the globalisation of the game. Today the Champions League isn't just the place to see the best European players; it's where you can watch the cream of the world's footballing talent. That's a big change. Not that watching a league game on a wet January night in Stoke can't be rewarding. It's just knowing that you can also tune in to Barcelona or Bayern Munich taking on Real

Madrid or Juventus, and see Argentina's Lionel Messi, Brazil's Neymar, Uruguay's Luis Suárez, Colombia's James Rodríguez or Chile's Arturo Vidal strut their stuff, that makes football more special. Football before the Champions League really was a different world.

It's not just the big teams and big players that are now more readily consumable to fans. It might not be fashionable to say it, but the Champions League, and the decision to expand the format to include the best runners-up as well as the domestic league champions, has introduced fans to a lot more teams in Europe. Before 1992, little was known about teams from less glamorous leagues; there was a passing interest if your team was playing them, but that was all, and chances were that these sides were knocked out of the competition pretty early. OK, the vast sums of money available to the traditional heavyweights still means that it's the big clubs that end up at the business end of things, but new and less fancied teams are elbowing their way into the picture, and for the fan who craves all things football, to have this access is incredible, even if occasionally your team finds itself on the wrong side of an upset.

FOOTBALL MOMENT

Inter Milan had not made a Champions League final for 38 years, therefore there was a huge pressure on the team. And myself! In addition, they were playing an extraordinary Barcelona, a team considered to be unbeatable. In fact, after 19 minutes Pedro scored for Barcelona. All my hopes were gone. But suddenly in the second half, after a first-half equalizer from Sneijder, they scored two more goals within 13 minutes, which led Inter to a 3–1 victory. I was over the moon and this feeling accompanied me until the end of that season as Inter managed to win the Champions League, the national title and the national cup. A Triple. Unbelievable!

Francesco, Italy

" *Football, bloody hell!* "

SIR ALEX FERGUSON ON WINNING THE CHAMPIONS LEAGUE FOR THE FIRST TIME WITH MANCHESTER UNITED

FOOTIE FACT

There is only one manager who has won the UEFA Champions League, the World Cup and the European Championship: Vicente del Bosque. He took Real Madrid to Champions League victory in 2000 and 2002, and won the World Cup and the European Championship with Spain in 2010 and 2012 respectively.

4

Only four players have won the Champions League in consecutive years. Step forward, French defender Marcel Desailly (Marseilles and AC Milan), Portuguese Paulo Sousa (Juventus and Dortmund), Spanish star Gerard Piqué (Manchester United and Barcelona) and Cameroon legend Samuel Eto'o (Barcelona and Inter Milan).

FOOTIE FACT

Swedish footballing force of nature Zlatan Ibrahimović was the first player to score for six clubs in the Champions League, but he has never won the competition despite playing for six clubs that have lifted the trophy: Ajax, Inter Milan, Barcelona, AC Milan, Juventus and Manchester United.

EUROPE'S BEST

It's a natural desire, almost an unconscious act, for the football fan to want to know who's the best in Europe, whether it's a player, a manager or a team. It's a debate that can fill a whole evening and still end in disagreement. It's a devil's advocate's dream of ifs, buts and maybes. How do you decide? Well, it makes sense to start with some ground rules.

Want to know who are Europe's best? Well, let's focus solely on the top competition, the Champions League, and let's consider achievements in the new competition on the same merit as those in the old European Cup.

WHO IS THE BEST TEAM?

If we're talking trophy wins, that simple: it's Spanish giants Real Madrid, winners on a record 11 occasions before the 2016–2017 competition, including a run of five consecutive triumphs between 1956 and 1960. The team closest to challenging the record of Los Blancos is AC Milan from Italy, victors on seven occasions. As for English teams, Liverpool have won it five times, Manchester United three times and Nottingham Forest twice (which were back-to-back victories in 1979 and 1980), while Chelsea and Aston Villa have got their hands on it once each.

HOW ABOUT MANAGERS?

The most successful manager in the competition is Liverpool's Bob Paisley who won the European Cup in 1977, 1978 and 1981. However, Pep Guardiola, José Mourinho or Carlo Ancelotti can equal the record if they steer a club to the trophy again, and given the clubs they are in charge of and the players and budgets at their disposal, you wouldn't bet against them doing so.

SO THAT LEAVES THE PLAYERS

Who has won the most trophies? One player stands alone on six wins: Real Madrid's Francisco Gento, who picked up winners' medals for the Spanish side between 1956 and 1960 and in 1966. As for modern-day players, Paolo Maldini can look back at five wins for AC Milan, with the last one coming 18 years after the first, while Clarence Seedorf, Samuel Eto'o, Lionel Messi, Xavi Hernández and Andrés Iniesta have four triumphs to their names, with the Dutch midfielder the only man in the competition's history to win the trophy with three different teams (Ajax, Real Madrid and AC Milan). The most successful English player? Step forward Liverpool defender Phil Neal with four wins in 1977, 1978, 1981 and 1984.

FOOTIE FACT

The last British manager to win the UEFA Champions League was Sir Alex Ferguson, who led Manchester United to victories in 1999 and 2008. Before that it was Liverpool boss Joe Fagan in 1984.

SCREEN ADDICTION

· ·

> " *If Everton were playing at the bottom of my garden,*
> *I'd shut the curtains.* "
>
> **BILL SHANKLY**

Watching football on the TV: it's an institution. Billions of people around the world spend countless hours glued to the action, whether huddled round small sets or big screens, at home, at a friend's or in the pub.

Today, we're inundated with choice when it comes to catching a game; it's not just a wealth of domestic matches that we can watch – we can settle in for 90 minutes of action from countless competitions taking place almost anywhere in the world. But it wasn't always thus.

TRYING TO TUNE IN

For anyone over 40, it doesn't seem that long ago that watching an English top-tier game live on the box was something of a luxury, with fans at the mercy of the financial demands of club chairmen and television executives. Back then, catching a

European game that wasn't the final was a testament to your ability to stay up late into the night, and your capacity to first endure the latest snooker action.

Watching World Cup games was different for this generation too: it was once the height of exoticism. Unreliable feeds from faraway lands beamed the jaw-dropping skills of unknown players directly into your living room. These matches really were a portal to another world: it was a thrill to be watching regardless of who was playing. The mix of excitement and curiosity of something so familiar yet so different was electrifying. These games were an education, a cultural event.

Of course, it's different now, thanks in no small part to Sky. The broadcast company's investment has transformed the way we watch football, from the way we tune in for live games and highlights to how we get the latest news and how we keep up with the latest scores.

The change in how we keep abreast of the goals rattling in on a Saturday afternoon is an apt illustration of the revolution that has occurred in televised football over the past 20 years. In the UK, we went from relying on Ceefax or Teletext, whose analogue technology had to be manually mined for updates, to Sky's all-singing and all-dancing *Soccer Saturday* phenomenon, with its panel of ex-pros discussing games that they can see but we can't, and its live updates from every ground in the country.

FOOTBALL MOMENT

Unlike Real Madrid, Barcelona does not have a history of memorable comebacks. Neither does it have the reputation of being a gritty team that will fight its way back into a game. But on the night of 12 March 1997, in the second leg of a Copa del Rey quarter-final against the Atlético Madrid of Radomir Antic (the team had won the double in 1996), Barcelona came back to grab the winner in the last minutes of the game. This was the night I was finally turned into a football fan.

Atlético started dominating the game and after 31 min were already three up, thanks to a hat-trick from Pantic. At half-time Bobby Robson, then manager of Barcelona, took off two centre backs and brought on two strikers. It was soon to have effect. Ronaldo scored his first of the night two minutes into the second half. His second was to come three minutes later. Yet, Pantic was still to chip in another in the 51st minute to make it 2–4. Barcelona kept trying and in the 68th and 72nd minutes Figo and Ronaldo were each to score a goal. With a score of 4–4 (6–6 on aggregate), Atlético were still through. Barcelona needed one more and that came via Pizzi's header in the 82nd. The pundit completely lost it and cried into his microphone: 'Pizzi, Pizzi, Pizzi, it's so good you came!'

Harald, Austria

A HISTORY OF FOOTBALL ON TV

1937   The first televised match in England: Arsenal v Arsenal Reserves

1938   The first televised international match: England v Scotland

1938   The first televised FA Cup final: Huddersfield Town v Preston North End

1955   The BBC launches its highlights show *Sports Special*

1960   The first live game is televised by ITV: Blackpool v Bolton Wanderers

1962   *Match of the Week* and *Shoot* highlights programmes appear on ITV

1964   *Match of the Day* debuts on BBC2

1968   *The Big Match* is unveiled by London Weekend Television

1966   The BBC and ITV show the World Cup final live

1969   The first colour edition of *Match of the Day* is broadcast

1970   The first Goal of the Month competition appears

1970   Chelsea v Leeds United attracts a record audience of 20 million viewers

1970   The first World Cup (in Mexico) is shown in colour

1971   Slow-motion replays are introduced

1983   The first live league game is shown since 1960: Tottenham Hotspur v Nottingham Forest

1992 The Premier League is formed and BSkyB buy the rights to show the games

1992 ITV starts screening live Champions League football

1992 Channel 4 begins showing live Italian Serie A football

1997 The first channel dedicated to a single football club is launched by Manchester United: MUTV

2003 Sky and ITV share Champions League football coverage

2004 Sunday night *Match of the Day 2* is launched by the BBC

2010 The first live Premier League game in 3D is screened by Sky

2013 The Champions League final draws a TV audience of 360 million

2014 The World Cup final in Brazil is watched by one billion people worldwide

2015 BT Sport gets exclusive rights to Champions League and Europa League football

2016 Viewing figures for the Euro 2016 final are expected to have hit 300 million

32.3

In 1966, England overcame a resilient West Germany to win the World Cup in a pulsating game at Wembley Stadium. Over 96,000 people crammed into the London ground to witness the Three Lions' historic moment. A staggering 32.3 million watched events unfold on the television.

THE VOICE OF FOOTBALL

Part of the fabric of football on the TV is the commentators. Their prose can be as memorable as the game they're describing; it can be what makes it memorable. There is no better example than the Kenneth Wolstenholme commentary on the 1966 World Cup final between England and West Germany. If you're English, regardless of the generation you belong to, his famous words, 'Some people are on the pitch... they think it's all over... it is now!', will forever be a reminder of English football's most glorious moment. These ones from Wolstenholme have just as much power: 'It is only twelve inches high... it is solid gold... and it undeniably means England are the champions of the world.'

Another one of Britain's football commentary greats is Brian Moore, whose injection of the words 'It's up for grabs now...' into the dying seconds of the battle for the 1989 first division title, in which Arsenal would score to dramatically snatch the crown from Liverpool's grasp, brilliantly defined the stomach-turning tension of what was unfolding before him and something that would become part of football folklore.

Of course, every country has its own favourites. When Bjørge Lillelien uttered the immortal words in 1981 on Norwegian television, 'Lord Nelson! Lord Beaverbrook! Sir Winston Churchill! Sir Anthony Eden! Clement Attlee! Henry Cooper! Lady Diana! Maggie Thatcher – can you hear me, Maggie Thatcher! Your boys took one hell of a beating! Your boys took one hell of a beating!', the popular commentator left no doubt as to how the Norwegians felt to beat England.

His outburst made him a hero, and not just in his native land: there are quite a few Scots who take great pleasure in remembering his words.

> ### FOOTIE FACT
>
> ....
>
> In 2007, Jacqui Oatley became the first woman to commentate on a football game on *Match of the Day*, describing the Premier League match between Fulham and Blackburn Rovers.

GAME TIME

Of course, we do more than just watch football on the screen; we play it as well. Today the football video games industry is a multi-billion-pound business; a high-tech 3D world of playing and managing that features real players and real-life action. It's a far cry from the first games played on the likes of the Atari, ZX Spectrum or Commodore 64 in the 1980s.

When it came to playing on the ZX Spectrum, getting to the start was an art of perseverance in itself, involving carefully loading the game, which meant inserting a tape into a cassette deck and waiting for what seemed like an eternity for the basic graphics to appear. If you bumped the tape player, you had to start the whole process again. And when it did load, decent action was at a premium – the early games were more about managing a team, with any playing options incredibly basic by today's standards. Yet for football-obsessed kids, they were still gripping and an enthralling way to while away hour after hour.

Of course, the advent of gaming technology only made football games more exciting. With the arrival of new computer systems, such as the Amiga and Nintendo, some arcade-style playing of football became possible, which for those used to rudimentary games, was a watershed moment. Fast forward and now the likes of the *FIFA* and *Pro Evolution Soccer* series, which are played on a host of consoles including the Nintendo Wii and 3DS, the PS4 and PSP, and the Xbox 360 and Xbox One, bestride the football video game world like giants, with adults as much as kids the main players.

The *Football Manager* title remains amazingly popular, showing that football fans are as eager to hone their management skills as they are their playing, especially if it means having the chance to lead your lower-league team to the type of domestic and European glory that would be out of reach in the real world. The technology and scope of the game has evolved incredibly since the days when the likes of Bryan Robson and Kenny Dalglish were favourite players, with its realism such that some diehard gamers have applied for actual football management positions. They didn't get them of course, but the joy of game: it's right there.

1981   Atari launches *Pelé's Soccer*

1982   The first *Football Manager* is available for the ZX Spectrum

1989   *Kick Off* with its arcade-style action arrives on the Amiga

1992   *Championship Manager* becomes a favourite on the PC

1993   *Sensible Soccer* makes a play for *Kick Off*'s crown

1994   2D football with *International Superstar Soccer* for the SNES

1994   The first 3D football with *Virtua Striker*

1997   *Premiership Manager 98* lets users manage a Premiership team

1998   *FIFA: Road to World Cup 98* is licensed by FIFA

2001   *Pro Evolution Soccer* makes its debut on the PS2

2013   *FIFA 14*, *Pro Evolution Soccer 2014* and *Football Manager 2014* are launched

2014   *FIFA 15* is launched and for the first time includes women footballers

2016   *FIFA 17* and *Pro Evolution Soccer 2017* arrive

FOOTIE FACT

According to the Guinness World Records, the record for the longest football video game marathon is 38 hours, 49 minutes and 13 seconds, set by Portuguese pair Marco Ramos and Efraim Ie on *Pro Evolution Soccer 2012* in November 2011.

FOOTBALL PLAYERS:
THE BEST OF THE BEST

∙∙∙

❝ Maradona good, Pelé better, George Best. ❞
FOOTBALL SAYING IN BELFAST, BIRTHPLACE OF GEORGE BEST

Trying to pick the best players isn't easy – just look at the state of a lot of fantasy football teams. Nevertheless it's something we're keen to do and we're not alone. Football loves a trophy and the game's governing bodies love to give them out, and the world's best player is an obvious accolade to reward. However, the prize is a relatively new one, a status that speaks to just how recent the globalisation of the game has been.

A GOLDEN BALL

In the beginning, there was a golden ball, the Ballon d'Or, a prize for the European Footballer of the Year conceived in 1956 by French football journalist Gabriel Hanot, shortly after he helped establish the European Cup, the forerunner of today's Champions League. The prize was voted for by journalists and was only open to European players appearing for European clubs. So, the likes of Pelé, Garrincha and Jairzinho weren't included. Nevertheless, the list of early winners still reads like a roll call of the world's greatest players.

The criteria changed in 1995 to include non-European players at clubs in Europe and then in 1997 to any player in the world, at which point the Ballon d'Or became a world's best player trophy in all but name. Unsurprisingly, South Americans became frequent winners. However, by this time, FIFA had got in on the act and launched its own World Player of the Year award, as voted for by the coaches and captains of international teams. While undoubtedly a lofty honour, the FIFA award, initially at least, didn't have the glamour of its more established counterpart. That said, its cachet did rise and in 2010 common sense prevailed, with the organisers of the two awards deciding to throw their lots in together and create the FIFA Ballon d'Or. For a few years, football had a singular award to recognise the best player on the planet and the battle for ownership of this stellar bauble was a straight fight between Argentina and Portugal, with the combat taking place largely in Spain.

However, in 2016, Ballon d'Or and FIFA decided to go their separate ways, with the divorce creating the prospect of two yearly awards again. So, more jollies and gongs for Lionel and Cristiano then.

ON TOP OF THE WORLD

The world's best player winners' board is currently dominated by Barcelona's Argentinian wizard Lionel Messi and Real

Madrid's Portuguese man marvel Cristiano Ronaldo. The last time anyone else won any of the top player awards was 2007. Messi alone has won the FIFA Ballon d'Or four times and the old FIFA gong and the original Ballon d'Or once in that time.

Back in those dim, distant days before Messi and Ronaldo made the award shows all a bit samey, multiple wins were a little thinner on the ground. This brings us neatly to the original Ronaldo (Ronaldo Luís Nazário de Lima), the Brazilian centre forward whose hearty appetite has become clear since he retired. In his trimmer days, he scored goals and bagged awards for fun, including the FIFA/Ballon d'Or double in 1997 and 2002. Another all-time great to notch up this double header was Zinedine Zidane, in 1998. He went on to win the FIFA award again in 2000 and 2003 – he may have bowed out, in more ways than one, with a single header (to the chest of Italian defender Marco Materazzi), but he was undoubtedly the greatest player of his generation and possibly a few others.

Before 1991, there was only one trophy available and repeat winners in this era were even rarer, which makes the feats of three-time Ballon d'Or victors Johan Cruyff, Michel Platini and Marco van Basten even more impressive. Can you separate these players? Not really, but van Basten also took home the second FIFA award in 1992, while Platini won the Ballon d'Or three years on the trot between 1983 and 1985. Which leaves Cruyff, and it wouldn't be right to put him at the bottom of this exclusive pile. Let's just say that he is one of the greatest players in the history of the game.

As for players who got their hands on the Ballon d'Or twice, the list is just as glittering, including Argentinian-cum-Colombian-cum-Spaniard Alfredo Di Stéfano, whose eagerness for passports eventually qualified him; Franz Beckenbauer, or 'Der Kaiser' to his compatriots and quite a few others; and Karl-Heinz Rummenigge, a scoring machine and perpetual trophy winner of the type Germany seems to produce regularly.

109

Who is the leading international goalscorer of all time? A South America magician? A European master? No, it's Iranian hero Ali Daei. During a senior career that lasted nearly 20 years and took in clubs such as Bayern Munich and Hertha Berlin, the gifted striker scored 109 goals in 149 games for his country. That's 25 more than Puskás and 32 more than Pelé.

ONE-TIME WINNERS

There are only a few countries for which producing world-class players is the norm rather than the exception. While Germany, Netherlands, France, Brazil and Italy have been hotbeds of talent and, as a result, world's best player awards, there are a handful of nations that have had the chance to celebrate a winner only once.

- Bulgaria – 1994, Hristo Stoichkov, Barcelona

- Denmark – 1997, Allan Simonsen, Borussia Mönchengladbach

- Hungary – 1967, Flórián Albert, Ferencváros

- Liberia – 1995, George Weah, AC Milan

- Ukraine – 2004, Andriy Shevchenko, AC Milan

THE BEST OF BRITISH

It started so well: the first Ballon d'Or was awarded to an Englishman: Stanley Matthews. After the hubris-hammering defeats to the USA at the 1950 World Cup and, more notably, at the hands of Ferenc Puskás' Hungary in 1953 and 1954, the English FA were no doubt over the moon to see English football back on top again. And the Blackpool outside right was a worthy winner: he is considered one of the greatest English exponents of the game and even at 38 in 1956, he still had another 12 years of professional football to play.

England had to wait ten years for another stellar performer, in World Cup winner Bobby Charlton, but the Scots didn't have to be quite so patient, with Manchester United's Denis Law voted top of pile in 1964. Another Red Devil, George Best, made it three British winners in five years, claiming the gong in 1967 on the back of his club side's triumph in the European Cup. Thereafter British football has had little to cheer about: its *Best* days were quite literally behind it, in terms of world's best player awards at least. Kevin Keegan did win back-to-back titles in the late 1970s, albeit playing for German team Hamburg, and the only British winner since was Liverpool's Michael Owen in 2001.

Will Britain have another champion to celebrate soon? A Welshman is the only realistic hope. Of the few players in with a shout of breaking the Messi-Ronaldo stranglehold, one is Cristiano's club mate Gareth Bale, who has almost single-handedly put Wales on the international footballing map and helps keep the Real Madrid trophy winning machine rumbling on.

> ## FOOTIE FACT
>
> *France Football* devised a Player of the Century award in 1999. The award, voted for by the previous Ballon d'Or winners, went to Pelé. Maradona came second and Johan Cruyff third.

974

Juventus goalkeeper Gianluigi Buffon holds the record for the longest run without conceding a goal in Italy's premier league, Serie A. After an Antonio Cassano goal on 10 January 2016, the Italian international No. 1 and World Cup winner wasn't beaten again until the Turin derby against Torino on 20 March 2016, a whopping 974 minutes of play later.

THE BEST WORST STARTS – FIVE DISASTROUS DEBUTS

Making a debut is a moment that players eagerly await. However, they don't always go to plan. Sometimes they go like a dream, sometimes they pass without notice and sometimes they are a complete and utter nightmare.

❶ JONATHAN WOODGATE V ATHLETIC BILBAO, LA LIGA 2005

Englishman Woodgate was one of Real Madrid's more low-key *galácticos*, but at £13.4 million he was still expected to make a big impact. And he did. Just not one he wanted. The injury-prone defender had to wait a year to make his debut and when he did, he was on the scoresheet within 25 minutes. But it was an own goal and a spectacular one at that – a diving header has rarely been executed so perfectly. To compound the misery, midway through the second half, the ex-Leeds player picked up his second yellow card, bringing his miserable maiden match to a premature end.

❷ LIONEL MESSI V HUNGARY, INTERNATIONAL FRIENDLY 2005

Even the world's best players can have stinkers and Messi had a big one in his first game for Argentina. After some U-20 World Cup heroics earlier in the year, Messi's senior international debut was much anticipated. It would come against Hungary and Messi would step on to the field at 64 minutes. He would step off it before the clock ticked round to 66. Straight into the action, Messi embarks on one of his trademark dribbles but Hungarian defender Vilmos Vanczák is pulling him back, seemingly intent swapping shirts earlier than usual. The diminutive Argentine tries to shrug the hulking Vanczák off, with his arm gently grazing his opponent's neck. The Hungarian goes down clutching his face like a sniper had got him from the crowd. The referee buys it and brandishes a red card to a stunned Messi.

FOOTBALL PLAYERS: THE BEST OF THE BEST

❸ JASON CROWE V BIRMINGHAM, ENGLISH LEAGUE CUP 1997

Crowe's career at Arsenal never amounted to much and no one would remember his time at the club if it weren't for the defender's debut. The English right back was no doubt keen to make an impression after getting a rare chance to play for the first team. He had the misfortune to be backup to the ever-dependable England international Lee Dixon, so it was important to make a big impact. He did but in all the wrong ways. Coming on in extra time in an English League Cup game against Birmingham City, the 19-year-old lasted a grand total of 33 seconds before receiving a red card for a wincingly high tackle. He would play just two more matches for the Gunners, neither of them as memorable as his first.

❹ ALI DIA V LEEDS UNITED, ENGLISH PREMIER LEAGUE 1996

There was no red card involved in Dia's debut, just a red face or two. Graeme Souness, manager of a struggling Southampton, thought his prayers had been answered. Out of the blue, former World Player of the Year George Weah had got in touch and tipped him off about his cousin Dia, a Senegalese international who had played for French giants Paris Saint-Germain. The south coast club duly gave him a month-long contract. Too good to be true? Oh yes. If anyone had bothered to check, they would have discovered that the whole story was a complete lie and Dia was a fake. But no one did. So the club's newest star gets a chance to shine against Leeds in a big Premier League game, coming on for injured talisman Matthew Le Tissier. Unsurprisingly, Dia is dire and wanders around very much like a player that is hopelessly out of his depth. But it still takes 22 minutes before a bewildered Souness substitutes his substitute.

⑤ STANLEY MILTON V STOCKPORT COUNTY, ENGLISH DIVISION THREE 1934

Sitting in the dressing room at half-time, goalkeeper Milton probably thought that his debut for Halifax Town wasn't going too badly. OK, his team were losing and he'd let in two goals, but it could have been worse. After all, high-scoring games were a regular occurrence at this time and his side were more than capable of turning the match around. Except that wasn't what happened. Something much more calamitous did. In the second half Milton picked the ball out of his net a confidence-destroying 11 times as Stockport racked up 13 unanswered goals. To add salt to the wound, the Hatter's striker Joe Hill, another debutant, bagged a hat-trick. This record for the heaviest football league defeat still stands today.

FOOTIE FACT

Swedish striking sensation Zlatan Ibrahimović has scored on his debut in the Champions League, Italy's Serie A, La Liga in Spain, France's Ligue 1 and the English Premier League. The goals came for Ajax, Juventus, Barcelona, Paris Saint-Germain and Manchester United. Dependable.

FOOTIE FACT

Nick Culkin's Manchester United career lasted mere seconds. Arsenal were entertaining the Old Trafford club in August 1999 and as the clock ticked into injury time at the end of the game, the Red Devils' goalkeeper Raimond van der Gouw received a boot in the face from an overly keen Gunner. After a lengthy delay, the Dutch stopper was replaced by Culkin. As soon as the replacement keeper put his boot through the ball to restart the game, the referee blew for full-time. Culkin never pulled on a United jersey again.

AROUND THE WORLD
IN FOOTBALL
TOURNAMENTS

> ❝ *A chap was once trying to get me to play for his club in America. 'We'll pay you $20,000 this year,' he said, 'and $30,000 next year.' 'OK,' I replied, 'I'll sign next year.'* ❞
> **GEORGE BEST**

One of the great football debates is 'what is the best league in the world?'. Is it the English Premier League? The Spanish La Liga? The German Bundesliga? The Italian Serie A or the French Ligue 1? But why stop there: is the UEFA Champions League better than the Asian, African or South American equivalents? And what about international competitions? How does the European Championship stack up against the Asian Football Confederation (AFC) Asian Cup, Africa Cup of Nations or the Copa América?

LEAGUE RIVALRY

Let's start with domestic football and assume that because Europe attracts the world's best players (based on the fact that European club players dominate world's best player awards), its top leagues are the best in the world. So, is it really possible to choose between them? The French league is certainly the *arriviste*: for a long time it existed in the shadow of its continental peers, but a colossal injection of cash from Qatari and Russian billionaires has put it in a new light. That said, the shine has dulled a little of late as the spending has slowed dramatically in the south. Nevertheless, the face of French football is very different thanks to Paris Saint-Germain.

But football teams having extraordinary amounts of money is not exactly a new phenomenon in European club football. The number of wealthy foreign investors in the English Premier League grows season by season. Chelsea's oligarch Roman Abramovich led the charge of the billionaire brigade and has been followed by Abu Dhabi's Sheikh Mansour at Manchester City, the American Glazer family at Old Trafford and John W. Henry at Liverpool. More recent reinforcements have had an Eastern flavour, including Thai duty-free billionaire Vichai Srivaddhanaprabha at Leicester and Iran's Farhad Moshiri at Everton, while the Chinese government has bought a chunk of Manchester's Blues. Talking of the People's Republic, a number of prominent Midlands clubs, including West Bromwich Albion and Aston Villa, have been snapped up by Chinese investors.

As for Italy, Indonesian tycoon Erick Thohir and then Chinese entrepreneur Zhang Jindong took over Inter Milan. Perhaps the lack of mega-rich foreign owners is what sets Spanish and

German football apart, for now at least, although Barcelona and Real Madrid are among the richest clubs in the world and throw their weight around in the transfer market accordingly: just look at Madrid's love for *galácticos* and Barça's ability to assemble its Messi-Suárez-Neymar strike force.

As for the German Bundesliga: Bayern Munich are undoubtedly a heavyweight but for the time being there isn't the same level of foreign money and it is notable that it is usually only Bayern that splash fantastic amounts of cash on players. That said, the arrival of Red Bull-backed RB Leipzig in the Bundesliga has put the cat among the pigeons. The energy-drink company has certainly given the East German team wings and it looks set to ruffle some footballing feathers thanks to the Austrian company's billions. For now, the Bundesliga remains famous for its low ticket prices.

How about styles of play? The English Premier League is known for its frenetic pace and valuing industry over ability, and for its physicality. Anyone who has grown up playing football in England and then taken to the field in Europe, at whatever level, will know that competing requires less muscularity and less contact.

The pace of football in Spain and Italy is traditionally slower, which when combined with the reduced physicality, supposedly gives a greater platform for players' technical ability. Just a stereotype? Well, look at the garlands Barcelona and Spain's possession-based game tiki-taka has received. Where does French and German football stand in all of this? Somewhere in between, with the former perhaps displaying a more continental style and the latter closer in complexion to the English game. However, as football comes increasingly to resemble one giant melting pot, with domestic leagues featuring players from every corner of the planet and with the idea of nationality and different nations' styles being subverted by this distribution of talent and the multinational heritage of a growing number of young players, these lines will blur further and it will be harder to apply any stereotypes. That said, the arguments are likely to go on just the same.

FOOTBALL MOMENT

Hamburg v IFK Goteborg in 1982, UEFA Cup final at Volkpark Stadion in Hamburg. The Germans were so sure of winning that they were selling scarves with 'Hamburg UEFA Cup winners 1982' printed on them. IFK (we) beat them 3–0 and took home Sweden's first international club title (the first leg we won 1–0 at Ullevi, Goteborg). Almost all Hamburg players were national team players, with the likes of Manfred Kaltz, Horst Hrubesch, Uli Stein and Felix Magath – simply a top team in Europe that went on to win the equivalent of the Champions League.

Anders, Sweden

FOOTIE FACT

When Leicester City won the Premier League in 2016, they became the first team outside of Manchester and London to win the top prize in English domestic football since Blackburn Rovers in 1995.

CONTINENTAL SHIFTS

If the UEFA Champions League is the Hollywood blockbuster that everyone and his dog knows about, the Copa Libertadores, the South American equivalent, is the indie star that despite being blessed with unbelievable quality can struggle to find a global audience. And what does that make the African Champions League? The art-house oddity? The no-budget surprise?

One thing is for certain when it comes to the African Champions League, while it may not have the riches, global viewing figures or all-star cast of its more illustrious compatriots, it is no less competitive or colourful. What challenges does the UEFA competition throw up for players? Well, for big-club players there are the occasional trips to smaller teams from less celebrated leagues whose changing rooms and pitches aren't as manicured as the ones they're used to, and for those not used to it, playing in inclement conditions in the outreaches of Eastern Europe must be something of an inconvenience. Also, there's the reality of playing important domestic games after just a couple of days rest. When it comes to the African Champions League, concerns are a little different. First of all, flying across Europe in club jets or those chartered from British Airways or the like is one thing, but criss-crossing Africa on airlines with less reassuring safety records is another altogether. Then there's the prevalence of war in Africa, which affects everything from travel and accommodation, to pitch conditions and the stability of spectators. Can you imagine how England, Spain or Italy's top players would deal with the need for 12-hour flying schedules to avoid warzones or armed soldiers running on the pitch to confront them about a tackle? Or how about voodoo in the form of blood sprinkled under seats? Or, thanks to rules that say home teams are responsible for the opposition's accommodation, having to stay in a hotel located in a red-light district whose noise prohibits rest even for the deepest of sleepers? Winning the UEFA Champions League is the ultimate test of a team? It's hard not to read about the African Champions League and think otherwise.

FOOTIE FACT

Who is the European Championship's top goalscorer? It's a tie between former French midfield maestro Michel Platini, who scored nine goals in a single tournament in 1984, and Portuguese scoring sensation Cristiano Ronaldo, who has racked up the same amount of strikes over four tournaments.

INTERNATIONAL BATTLE

When it comes to regional international tournaments, the European Championship, the Africa Cup of Nations and the Copa América are the big ones. Being champions of Europe, Africa or South America is as big as it sounds.

The Copa América arguably has the grandest game of them all: Brazil against Argentina, a clash whose history and talented combatants rarely make it anything other than explosive. Getting one over on the old enemy means as much in South America as it does anywhere else. That's not to the say the rest of the teams are makeweights: Uruguay are frequent apple-cart upsetters, winning the tournament in 2011 and holding the record for most trophies going into the 2019 competition, and the regular inclusion of top teams from Central and North America, such as Mexico and the USA, also keeps things interesting.

The big guns in the Africa Cup of Nations are the likes of Egypt, Nigeria, Cameroon, Ghana and the Ivory Coast. Before 2017, between themselves, this group has taken the trophy home on 19 occasions since the first tournament in 1957, with Egypt the top dog by some distance with seven victories, including three in a row in the 2000s. But that doesn't mean the title hasn't been shared around: only as recently as 2012, when the competition was held in Gabon and Equatorial Guinea, the unfancied Zambia team beat favourite Ivory Coast 8–7 on penalties in the final. David beat Goliath.

As for the European Championship, Iberia has had a stranglehold on this trophy for a while now, with Spain winning in 2008 and 2012, and Portugal taking the trophy in 2016, but this competition has thrown up its fair share of surprises in the past 20 years or so. The Danes walked off the beach to the claim the title in 1992 and Greece ripped the form book to shreds in 2004. The records show both have been European champions. Which is more than England can claim.

22

If the final of the 1960 European Championship was replayed today, the game would feature 22 teams. The match that drew the inaugural tournament to a close was contested by the Soviet Union and Yugoslavia. This communist tête-à-tête ended in a 2–1 victory for the Soviets, courtesy of an extra time-winner from Viktor Ponedelnik.

FOOTIE FACT

Former Valencia, Villarreal and Sevilla goalkeeper Andrés Palop won the European Championship with Spain in 2008 without ever earning an international cap.

LIFE AFTER FOOTBALL

❝ *Tell him he's Pelé and get him back on.* **❞**

PARTICK THISTLE MANAGER JOHN LAMBIE ON BEING TOLD BY THE PHYSIO THAT HIS
STRIKER COLIN MCGLASHAN HAD SUFFERED CONCUSSION AND DIDN'T KNOW WHO HE WAS

A life without football: a chilling thought if there ever was one. For players, even the longest careers have to come to an end. And then what? Naturally, football being football, just because a player is retired doesn't mean there isn't an interest in what they're up to. The decision to swap playing for managing retains a timeless popularity, but if a footballer is loath to stray too far from pitchside, today there are other options: never have the professions of commentator, pundit and presenter been so populated with former players. But once, it wasn't the commentator's microphone or the pundit's chair that most appealed, but the other side of the bar, with owning a pub a much preferred retirement plan. Of course, there are those who bucked the trend.

THE LONGEST FOOTBALLING CAREERS

Whether Arsène Wenger deserves all the credit or not, footballers' careers are much longer today thanks to the change in attitude to eating and drinking that he, at the very least, helped introduce. From the mid-1990s, when the French manager took charge of Arsenal, discussion of footballers' diets no longer focused solely on industrial quantities of lager and steak and chips.

Gradually it became acceptable to talk about pasta, steamed meat, vegetables and rice, and having only the occasional beer. Today, strict diets are part and parcel of a top player's life – Ryan Giggs gave up butter on his toast to help extend his playing career – and being teetotal, at least during the season, is increasingly common. In the modern Premier League era, turning up to training smelling like a brewery is an offence that will most likely find you dropped and fined, but you don't need to go back too many years to find tales of players kicking off while half-cut. It isn't much wonder that careers were much shorter in the days before Wenger.

Giggs is a good example of this revolution. The Welsh Wizard finally hung up his boots at the end of the 2013–2014 season, bringing to an end at the age of 40 a glittering 24-year career. He equalled Paolo Maldini, who retired at 41 having played 24 seasons for AC Milan and Italy, and also won a mantelpiece full of top honours. Other receivers of notable long-service awards include Maldini's teammate Franco Baresi, a sweeper for 20 years at the Rossoneri; Francesco Totti, who has been playing in Serie A for AS Roma's first team for 22 years; Jack Charlton, who shored up Leeds United's defence between 1953 and 1972;

and Paul Scholes, who drove Manchester United's midfield for 20 years from 1993 to 2013.

However, none of them can match Stanley Matthews, whose senior playing career spanned 37 years, with the famous outside right competing at the top level until 1965 when he was 50. It can't be a coincidence that the Magician, as he was known, was teetotal, a vegetarian and a non-smoker.

FOOTIE FACT

Former goalkeeper Peter Shilton made 1,390 appearances during his career, which included 1,005 league games in England. He also holds the record number of England caps, at 125.

12

Former England goalkeeper Richard Wright retired in 2016 and he can look back on a career that includes two English Premier League titles. What makes this so special? It took him just 12 games to earn the medals – for Arsenal in 2001–2002 (12 appearances) and for Manchester City in 2013–2014 (0 appearances). His brief stint in north London also saw him pick up a FA Cup winners' medal.

FOOTBALL BOOTS TO MANAGERS' SUITS

Swapping the pitch for the dugout has long been a chosen career path for players throughout the game, and time has shown that brilliance with the ball still remains no indicator of managerial aptitude. That's not to say the efforts of these institutionalised souls haven't added something joyful to the game, whether they've flourished or failed.

Roy Keane isn't everyone's cup of tea, but he is universally regarded as one of the best players of his generation. A midfield maestro and menace combined in one gloriously effective footballer. Yet managerial life hasn't been kind to him: it all started so well at Sunderland before ending in barbed comments and resignation amid a run of poor results. And the less said about his tenure at Ipswich Town the better. Another outstanding footballer unable to match success on the pitch to that off it is Holland's Ruud Gullit, whose prowess on the field earned an incredible haul of medals but whose ability in the dugout hasn't been so illustrious, including being sacked by Chelsea and Newcastle United. It's still early days for Gary Neville, but the much-respected pundit had his fingers seriously burnt at Valencia. His managerial reign in Spain lasted just a few painful months: he lost his first nine games and won just three of the 16 that he would eventually oversee. He took the side out of the Champions League and the Europa League, and suffered a 7–0 thumping in the Spanish league cup. So calamitous was the experience that the former England and Manchester United defender has said he may never coach again. Ouch.

However, failing to transfer mastery on the field to success in the manager's seat is by no means a modern phenomenon. Step forward World Cup-winning hero Sir Bobby Charlton, who took up a role of player–manager at Preston North End after his time at Manchester United. He steered the team to relegation in his first season and it wasn't long after that he thought better of management altogether, never to take up such a role again.

Of the top footballers that have made a success of management, perhaps the best advertisement for the ex-player is Pep Guardiola. While his managerial star is burning the brightest of all at the moment, breathing new life into Manchester City after safeguarding Bayern Munich's imperiousness and leading Barcelona to unprecedented success, it shouldn't be forgotten that before he stepped into his manager's shoes, his boots were helping to orchestrate the midfield at the Camp Nou.

Another star player–star manager is Carlo Ancelotti. At club level he captained Roma to an Italian championship and four Coppa Italia trophies, and at AC Milan, he was part of one of the best teams of the time, winning back-to-back European Cups in 1989 and 1990 alongside the likes of Marco van Basten, Ruud Gullit, Frank Rijkaard, Paolo Maldini and Franco Baresi. Incredibly, his managerial career has been even more glittering, winning top-flight league championships in the Premier League, Serie A and Ligue 1 with Chelsea, AC Milan and Paris Saint-Germain respectively, as well as three Champions Leagues (two with the Italian team and the other with Real Madrid). Having stepped into the managerial hot seat at Bayern Munich in 2016, only a fool would bet against him adding to his illustrious haul.

UNUSUAL RETIREMENTS

When they hang up their boots, not all footballers follow the path into the managerial or media worlds. A few have ended up in some more unusual post-career professions. If anything, knowing that some players end up doing more ordinary jobs makes them all the more likable, a bit more like one of us.

Perhaps the most famous member of this club is former Swedish international Tomas Brolin. Known once to his country and Leeds United fans as a striking wunderkind, his reputation has rather been taken over by his exploits in retirement. He has been involved in selling shoes, vacuum cleaners and properties in Sweden, and has tried his hand at being a restaurateur, as well as making a pop record with 1990s flash-in-the-pan Dr Alban. Staying in Scandinavia, former Danish international PSV Eindhoven player Ivan Nielsen decided to become a plumber, while Brolin's fellow Swede and ex-Sheffield Wednesday star Klas Ingesson chose a life as a lumberjack.

English football is full of such stories as well. England World Cup winner Ray Wilson worked as an undertaker when he gave up the game and former England midfielder Neil Webb became a postman on retirement. More recently, ex-journeyman striker Brett Angell spent some time stacking shelves at a well-known supermarket (before going on to coach in New Zealand). Clearly, every little helped.

Of course, a retirement job out of the game doesn't always mean one of out the glare of the camera and press. Eric Cantona swapped the Theatre of Dreams for treading actual boards, appearing in films including *Elizabeth* and *Looking for Eric*. If the transformation of the enigmatic Frenchman from star player to film star didn't surprise too many, the same move by footballing hard man Vinnie Jones certainly did. Indeed, he has arguably found more success in front of the camera than in front of a back four, with roles in *Lock, Stock and Two Smoking Barrels*, *Snatch* and *X-Men: The Last Stand* to name but a few. Football: it's a funny old game.

THE FINAL WHISTLE

> *Winning isn't everything. There should be no conceit in victory and no despair in defeat.*
> **SIR MATT BUSBY**

So, the final whistle is near. The fat lady is about to sing. Fergie time can't last forever. Except it isn't, she won't and in a way it can. These stories and statistics, musings and mutterings are just the tip of the iceberg. Football is full of stories: weird, wonderful, terrifying and tragic.

Pierce the venal corporate veneer of the modern game and burrow beneath its gambling greased skin and you'll find a rich seam of heart-warming, heart-stopping and heart-rending tales. Each one laced with names and numbers, famous and infamous. The top leagues and elite competitions are a goldmine, but don't stop there because every country in the world has its own history of football, its own long list of deeds done in the name of this sport. It makes addictive reading.

And football is a gift that will always keep giving. More wonder goals will be scored, penalties missed, records set, rules broken, rivalries forged, tempers lost, red cards earned, trophies won and history made. The game will change and the game will stay the same. There will be more earth-shattering victories, astonishing come backs, unbelievable upsets and unexpected collapses. Players, managers and teams will continue to live up to reputations and to confound expectations. Administrators will continue to meddle, misuse and misappropriate. Each twist and turn will remind us why we've become so addicted and are happy to stay that way. We'll always be ready to cling to the next bit of magic or madness that comes our way.

We'll keep turning up, turning out and turning on. We won't stop watching, listening, reading and writing. We'll always be there, waving, singing, shouting, cheering and crying. And we'll be doing it for the love of football.

> *What is a club in any case? Not the buildings or the directors or the people who are paid to represent it. It's not the television contracts, get-out clauses, marketing departments or executive boxes. It's the noise, the passion, the feeling of belonging, the pride in your city. It's a small boy clambering up stadium steps for the very first time, gripping his father's hand, gawping at that hallowed stretch of turf beneath him and, without being able to do a thing about it, falling in love.*

SIR BOBBY ROBSON

ACKNOWLEDGEMENTS

Special thanks to Ivan Restrepo for keeping the dream alive. I would also like to thank Francesco Valentino, Marko Van Waveren, Cicioc Bogdan-Gheorghe, Warren Hokan, Harald Pedro Langer Sy-Quia, Giovanni Gallo, Victor Montserrat-Ortiz, Fernando Russo, Umidjon Rakhmonberdiev, Anders Isaksson, Ahmad Mazrui and Jan Kooy.

If you're interested in finding out more about our books,
find us on Facebook at **Summersdale Publishers**
and follow us on Twitter at **@Summersdale**

www.summersdale.com

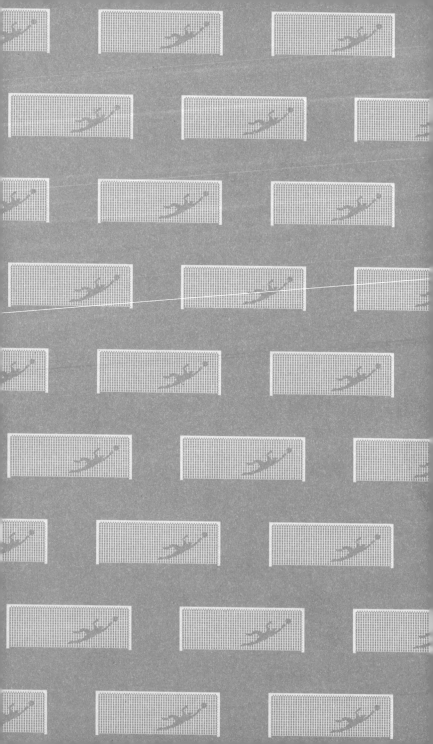